Dedicated to
my husband, Pol, whose sensitivity to language
and patience in proofreading contributed to the clarity
of concepts and terms

Contents

Preface

Dance Composition Basics: Capturing the Choreographer's Craft is designed for beginning courses in dance composition. The book introduces dancers to the craft of choreography through a series of problem-solving activities. Dancers of all styles from ballet to modern to jazz will find this book useful. The lesson activities and choreographic studies are designed as starting points to encourage novice dancers to embark on their own attempts at choreography.

In 30 years of working with dance students at the university level and in training dance educators for public schools, I have tried many different approaches to encourage student engagement in the choreographic process. Recently, I felt the need to look at current choreographic practice more closely and to use choreographic forms and devices in the same way that the current generation of choreographers is using them. In 1998, I approached Alain Charron, director of education at North Carolina Dance Theatre, with a plan. I proposed that we develop a series of grant projects that would enable me to study current choreographers at work while they created original dances for the North Carolina Dance Theatre. Alain and the North Carolina Dance Theatre agreed to develop the projects. The compositional activities in this book evolved as a result of this partnership, which spanned six years of study and five separate grant awards from the North Carolina Arts Council. I have featured two of the noted choreographers whose work I analyzed, Alonzo King and Dwight Rhoden, in the text. This book does not attempt to include all dance concepts or all choreographic forms; it is limited to those operations and forms used by King and Rhoden to create three original works: *Chants* and *Dreamer* by King and *Verge* by Rhoden. Thus, the works themselves as they were created determined the compositional exercises of the book.

We began our work with King, who created *Chants* in 1998 and *Dreamer* in 1999. Three years later, in 2002, we completed a similar project with Rhoden, who choreographed the ballet *Verge.* While each choreographer was in the process of creating his dance, I was allowed to attend every rehearsal and take notes and hold interviews as needed in order to capture the choreographic decisions. After spending the day in the studio, I would go home and translate the process I witnessed into lessons of graduated difficulty. By analyzing the different choreographic concepts I had just seen, I was able to break down and sequence choreographic tasks.

Organization

The book is divided into five chapters: chapter 1, The Body: Exploring the Ways We Move; chapter 2, Space: Exploring the Expanse We Move In; chapter 3, Time: Exploring Tempo; chapter 4, Energy: Force Generating Movement; and chapter 5, Choreographic Devices: Creating Finished Compositions. Each chapter features several lessons based on the choreographic concept highlighted in the chapter title. Each lesson includes the following sections:

- The **Vocabulary** list guides presentation and alerts the reader to key terms in the lesson.
- The **Introductory Statement** provides background information.
- The **Warm-Up** consists of movements designed to warm up the body and focus the mind to prepare for more complicated technical work. In most of the lessons, the warm-up movement directly relates to the material to be covered in the Structured Improvisations.
- **Structured Improvisations** are a series of improvisations designed to lead dancers to an understanding of the movement concepts of the lesson before they begin to create their own movement studies. The materials and motifs developed in the improvisations can be assembled later into more complex choreographic structures. Several different improvisational structures may be introduced in one lesson in order to provide dancers with different movement ideas. Each improvisation will result in a short movement phrase speaking to a specific concept. Dancers and instructors may choose which improvisations to use. A group or class of dancers participates in the improvisations as a whole, directed by an instructor or leader.
- **Problem Solving** is designed to allow dancers to apply the concepts presented in the improvisations to a work of their own. Dancers work alone or in small groups to complete a choreographic study that reflects the concepts presented in the lesson.
- **Discussion Questions** are questions to ponder while engaging in a problem-solving activity or watching selected video examples. They also introduce concepts that guided the choreographer.
- **Assessment Rubrics** allow for assessment of each dancer's learning. Each lesson culminates with a choreographic problem for dancers to solve by creating a short movement study. The Assessment Rubrics provided with each lesson are presented in a checklist format and introduce a common language and criteria for evaluating each study. The rubrics provide starting points for an instructor and peers to give relevant feedback and to perform verbal or written self-assessments. Each Assessment Rubric begins with Creating: Perceptual Skills, which describes the choreographic process and components of the study. This section is followed by Performing: Technical and Expressive Skills, which addresses the ability of the performer–creator to interpret and perform the study with clarity and accuracy. Finally, self-reflection is encouraged in the last section of the assessment, Responding: Intellectual and Reflective Skills. These rubrics were influenced by the National Assessments of Educational Progress (NAEP).

The rubrics offer a shorthand chart to assist in evaluating dancers' work, using the same criteria for each study. In addition, the rubrics may be copied and distributed to peers to assist dancers in giving accurate and useful feedback and to teach the ability to look at the construction of dance phrases.

Glossary

The glossary provides thumbnail definitions of the vocabulary terms listed at the beginning of each lesson. The definitions are given from a dancer's point of view as appropriate for each lesson. The glossary is designed to provide a working vocabulary for instructors and dancers to use while discussing or assessing work.

DVD

A DVD is included that documents each choreographic operation and allows students to observe a direct relationship between the activities in the dance composition classroom and current practices in the profession of dance. Because the assigned studies relate directly to the masterworks choreographed by King and Rhoden, many examples featured in the DVD show each choreographer working on the same movement problems featured in a lesson. Students will see the choreographer in action with professional dancers as he develops the movement material for his dance. Choreographic operations from the lessons are modeled in the studio as the choreographer works with the dancers. Students of composition can see a choreographer working with professional dancers, struggling with the same creative problems that they have been assigned. See How to Use the DVD on page xv and the DVD menu on page xvii for more information.

Beginning students in dance composition thus can explore choreographic craft by first being introduced to a concept intellectually through discussion, questioning, and video examples of a professional choreographer. Afterward, they explore simple movement ideas to discover a movement vocabulary and original dance phrases through structured improvisations. They then develop their movement ideas into a longer study with a more specific movement problem to solve. Last, students, peers, and the instructor provide feedback and assess each original movement study.

Concluding Remarks

In 1989, Stuart Hodes, former principal dancer with the Martha Graham Dance Company and current school advisor for the Martha Graham School in New York City, wrote an article titled "Transforming Dance History: The Lost History of Rehearsals." In this article, Hodes argued that the history of modern dance as an art form has been written in the studio, where the major choreographers of the 20th century created the works that became the masterpieces for successive generations of dancers. I would argue that the new trends in choreography are found in the same way—in the rehearsal studio, as the next generation of choreographers creates new work.

Currently, choreographers combine dance influences as needed to serve a choreographic vision. Choreographers draw from whatever movement source is available. As well, dancers no longer train exclusively in one style of dance. Many contemporary dance companies have become repertory companies. The works performed vary in style, and different choreographers and dance styles are often featured in one evening's performance.

With so many disparate influences affecting dance and dance creation, the goal of this book is to introduce students of dance composition to some of the compositional structures used by professional choreographers today. Through carefully designed lessons, students use these structures as models as they take their first steps into the craft of choreography.

Featured Artists and Works

Alonzo King

Alonzo King has works in the repertories of companies throughout the world including Frankfurt Ballet, Alvin Ailey American Dance Theater, Hong Kong Ballet, North Carolina Dance Theatre, Joffrey Ballet, Dance Theater of Harlem, Washington Ballet, and many more. He has worked extensively in opera, television, and film and has choreographed works for prima ballerina Natalia Makarova and film star Patrick Swayze.

Renowned for his skill as a teacher, Mr. King has been guest ballet master for National Ballet of Canada, Les Ballets de Monte Carlo, San Francisco Ballet, Ballet Rambert, Ballet West, and others. In 1982, Mr. King founded Alonzo King's LINES Ballet, which has developed into an international touring company.

He has had numerous collaborations with outstanding musicians, such as legendary jazz great Pharoah Sanders; India's national treasure Zakir Hussain; Bernice Johnson Reagon, founder of Sweet Honey in the Rock; Nubian Oud Master Hamza al Din; and Polish composer Pavel Syzmanski.

In 1989, Alonzo King inaugurated the San Francisco Dance Center, which has grown into one of the largest dance facilities on the West Coast, and in 2002 he started the LINES Ballet School and Pre-Professional Program.

Elisabeth Fall

Alonzo King

In 1997, funded by National Endowment for the Arts and North Carolina Arts Council grants, King was engaged by North Carolina Dance Theatre to create four new ballets for the company over a period of four years. He began with *Map* (1997), followed by *Chants* (1998), *Dreamer* (1999), and *Tangos* (2000).

Alonzo King is a recipient of the NEA Choreographer's Fellowship, Irvine Fellowship in Dance, and grants from the National Dance Project and the National Dance Residency Program. He has received four Isadora Duncan Awards, the Hero Award from Union Bank, Los Angeles' Lehman Award, and the Excellence Award from KGO in San Francisco. He has served on panels for the National Endowment for the Arts, California Arts Council, City of Columbus Arts Council, and Lila Wallace-Reader's Digest Arts Partners Program.

He is a former commissioner for the city and county of San Francisco and a writer and lecturer on the art of dance. In 2005 King was awarded an honorary doctorate from Dominican University in San Rafael, California, and received New York's prestigious BESSIE award for choreography. His next commission is with the Royal Swedish Ballet.

About Chants

Chants is a suite of dances inspired by traditional music from Zaire, Guinea, Senegal, and Kenya. The work does not have a narrative line but rather reflects the mood of the music. King began the rehearsal process by explaining to the dancers that he believes the body to be an instrument making its own musical line that plays along with the musical score. It has its own individual rhythms and phrasing. Dancers make music with their bodies.

The work begins with the full company entering and exiting the dance space with movement that is reminiscent of animals as they congregate at a watering hole first thing in the morning. After introducing the cast, the ballet unfolds in a series of duets, solos, and small-group sections, each with its own personality inspired by the chosen chant. Images of play, games, and challenges present themselves as the dancers and choreography create poignant visual images.

About Dreamer

Dreamer was created to a piece of classical music by Alan Hovhaness called *Mysterious Mountain.* The dance work is inspired by the music but has a separate theme. King chose a teaching from Hindu belief stating that the world exists in equilibrium between three *gunas,* or categories of existence.

- The first guna is Tamas, or inertia, which opposes action and produces darkness and heaviness (ignorance).
- The second is Rajas, or activity, energy, and dynamism (action).
- The third is Sattva, or intellect, purity of knowledge, and enlightenment (wisdom).

These natural forces are personified in the dance and each human motivator is given a dynamic movement quality that defines the attribute of the guna. King uses Hindu religious thought as a point of departure and metaphor for the process of artistic creation. In the work, he introduces the germinal idea or dream that will be acted upon by the three natural forces in order to complete its creation. The motivation for the ballet is defining and understanding energy and its role in human self-actualization or creation. The ballet tells the story of the act of creation from its beginning in a dream to its fruition in actualization as it is aided by the forces of Tamas (inertia), Rajas (energy), and Sattva (wisdom and balance).

Energy, or the "texture in between," as King explains it, is the motivator of this work. King taught all movement immediately from its energy definitions. Actual movements by themselves were defined in energy first and then identified in shape and technique. King specifically defines energy as a combination of force and time.

EXAMPLE 1: Getting to Know Alonzo King

Featured Artists and Works

Dwight Rhoden

A native of Dayton, Ohio, Dwight Rhoden began dancing at the age of 17 while studying acting. He has performed with the Dayton Contemporary Dance Company and Les Ballet Jazz De Montreal, and was a principal dancer with the Alvin Ailey American Dance Theater. He has appeared in numerous television specials, documentaries, and commercials throughout the United States, Canada, and Europe, and has been a featured performer on many PBS Great Performances specials.

Dwight Rhoden

Rhoden has dedicated the past 10 years to the development of the critically acclaimed Complexions, Inc., which he codirects with Desmond Richardson. From the ground up, they have built an arts organization, produced numerous New York seasons, and toured extensively internationally with a roster of highly acclaimed artists. Rhoden has created more than 30 ballets for Complexions in addition to numerous other commissions. Together, Rhoden and Richardson have worked with, coached, and created for some of the most diverse artists in ballet and contemporary dance. They have used dance and multimedia to express their creative passion and universal message of diversity and unity of all art forms and people.

Rhoden's work has been presented by Lincoln Center's Alice Tully Hall, the Joyce Theatre, the Brooklyn Academy of Music, Majestic Theatre, the New Orleans Ballet Association, the Paramount Theater in Seattle, Isle de Dance Festival in Paris, Brazil's Festival of Arts, Maison de la Dance in France, numerous dance festivals in Italy, the Holland Dance Festival, Encore 2000, the Steps Festival in Switzerland, Festival of Las Palmas of the Canary Islands in Spain, Avery Fisher Hall Presents Lena Horne, the Children's Defense Fund Gala, Italy's Festival of Dance in Rome, and other venues across the United States, Europe, and South America. Rhoden has created works for numerous companies including the Alvin Ailey American Dance Theater, the Pennsylvania Ballet, the Joffrey Ballet, Phoenix Dance Company, Dayton Contemporary Dance Company, Philadanco, the Aspen Santa Fe Ballet Company, the Pittsburgh Ballet Theatre, and the Washington Ballet. He has served as artistic director of *A Celebration of Dance,* a company of principal dancers from American Ballet Theatre, Alvin Ailey, the Dance Theater of Harlem, and the Joffrey Ballet.

Rhoden has lectured and served as artist in residence at universities around the country. His collaboration with Prince, "Rave Unto the Year 2000," was aired on pay-per-view television. His current commissions include the New York City Ballet Diamond Project Choreographic Institute, the Dance Theater of Harlem, the Alvin Ailey American Dance Theater, and the Aspen Santa Fe Ballet Company. Rhoden is currently working on a film being produced by Patrick Swayze. He enjoys acting, writing poetry and lyrics, and performing in new and exciting productions. Rhoden is a 1998 New York Foundation for the Arts Award recipient and is currently guest artist in residence for the Dayton Contemporary Dance Company.

***About** Verge*

Verge starts with a solo for a character called the Impulse. He possesses all of the qualities of success and achievement that the rest of the dancers in the cast will try to achieve for the next 26 minutes of the ballet. The stage set is a huge target with a red center representing the goals everyone is shooting for, the bull's-eye, achieving the actual fruit. After the initial solo, the group is introduced, led by a character called the Alter Ego, who like a trickster tries to detract the dancers and the Impulse from their goals. The group is on the "verge" of success, so they must continue their quest slowly, getting closer and closer to the goal. Continuing toward the goal takes courage. Emotionally, the dance is really about finding that courage to follow a dream. There are six sections in *Verge*: The Impulse, Hypothetical Nuance, The If & Or Of It, Duplicitous Ironies, Pass Gradually Into, and Nirvana. In each of the first five sections the group led by Impulse moves toward its goals. In the last section, Nirvana, the whole group finally achieves them, and the ballet ends with the Impulse in the center, supported by his Alter Ego, with all of the dancers forming a circle around them. They have all become the "hot center." The goal is achieved.

"What gave you the idea to create this dance?"

Question to Dwight Rhoden from a student, Quail Hollow Middle School, Charlotte, North Carolina

"I don't know exactly why I started to create it, but I did come here with a concept. I think it had to do with something we all can relate to. Having an idea that you want to go for something . . . having a goal and then maybe having insecurity or maybe having an anticipation of getting there . . . having an anxiety of going for it . . . having some fear or some courage. So I decided, why not put this into a dance." May 2, 2003

EXAMPLE 2: Getting to Know Dwight Rhoden

How to Use the DVD

To guide your use of the DVD, icons have been placed throughout the book referring to further information on the DVD. They look like this:

EXAMPLE: Chapter 1, Lesson 1B: Defining "Impulse"

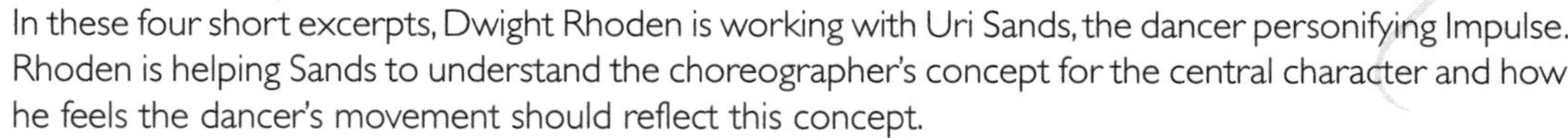

In these four short excerpts, Dwight Rhoden is working with Uri Sands, the dancer personifying Impulse. Rhoden is helping Sands to understand the choreographer's concept for the central character and how he feels the dancer's movement should reflect this concept.

The first line of the DVD example shows where to find it on the DVD. In this case, it is chapter 1, lesson 1B. The second part of the example provides a short description of what you will view.

The DVD is organized like the book. The main menu of the DVD corresponds with the five chapters of the book. A credits section and a featured artists and works section also are included on the main menu. The complete DVD menu can be found on pages xvii-xviii of the book.

To get started, place the DVD in your DVD player or DVD-ROM drive. From the main menu, select one of the chapters. A submenu will appear with the chapters listed on the left and the lessons of the selected chapter on the right. These lessons refer to the DVD examples found throughout the book. Select one of the lessons to view the DVD example. After the selected DVD example plays, the DVD automatically returns to the submenu with the next lesson of the chapter highlighted.

The best way to use the DVD is to view the DVD examples mentioned within each lesson in the book. When a lesson refers to a DVD example, reviewing it will provide further insight into the choreographic problem to be solved.

Dance Composition Basics DVD Menu

Acknowledgments

This book could not have been written without the collaboration of North Carolina Dance Theatre and its artistic director Jean-Pierre Bonnefoux; its education directors, the late Alain Charron and its subsequent director Ambre Emory Maier; and its corps of highly trained dancers featured on the DVD and in the photos throughout the book. They endured my many hours of sitting in corners of the studio as I jotted down copious notes and drew pathways and symbols to help me remember formations or rhythms that just might find themselves in a lesson.

A special note of thanks must go to both Alonzo King and Dwight Rhoden, who generously consented to this scrutiny of their choreographic processes. Both men were exceedingly helpful and amazingly clear and respectful of us all while they worked.

A special note of acknowledgment must go to Stuart Grasberg, the videographer who was responsible for filming all of the video examples used in the accompanying DVD. He was at my side with his "camera eye," catching as many of the details of the creative process as time and energy allowed.

Last but not least, I must thank the public school dance educators, many of my former students, and my current students in dance education, who field-tested lessons and served as my laboratory for trying out lesson formats and choreographic problems.

The Body: Exploring the Ways We Move

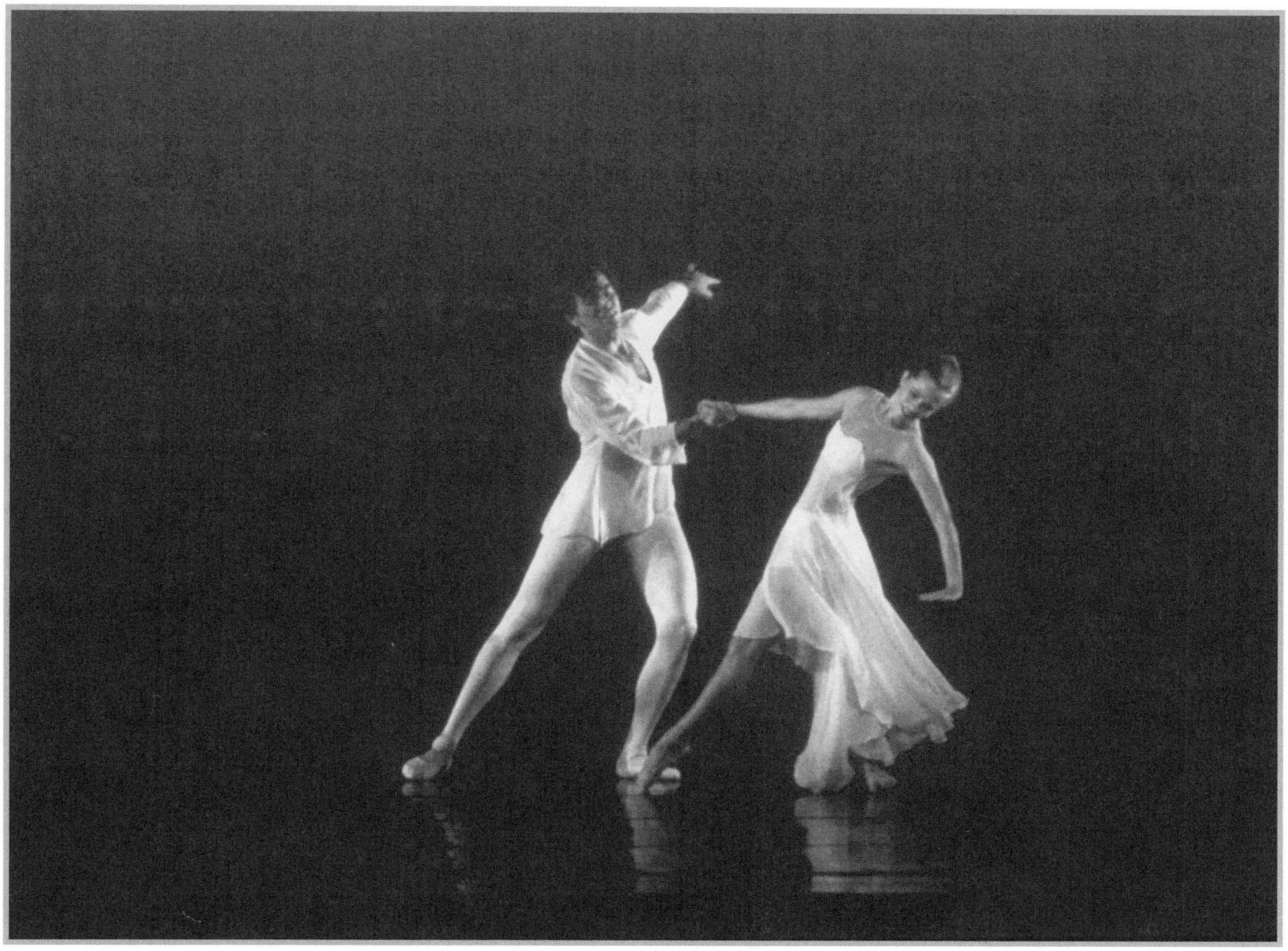

Mia Cunningham as the Dreamer (symbolizing creative thought) being guided by Hernan Justo as Sattva (enlightenment) from Alonzo King's dance work *Dreamer.*

OVERVIEW

Dance uses the body as an instrument of expression in time and space. Behind every movement lies an intention that is revealed by conscious control of energy. It is the choreographer's job to design dance compositions that manipulate body shape and movement patterns creatively in space and in time with a determined energy. This manipulation makes the choreographer's emotions and aesthetic inventions concrete, and draws in the emotional participation of the performers and the viewers of the choreographer's creation.

This chapter explores the ways we move our bodies in choreography by looking at the range of movement; the coordination of movement from the inside out; locomotion using action words; and the choreographic use of personal space, nonlocomotor movement, gestures, and shapes. The goal is to facilitate the development of movement phrases or motifs that can be expanded into solo studies. Each movement concept is introduced with a structured improvisation, followed by a larger creative problem to solve. Video recordings in the rehearsal studio document the creative processes of choreographers Dwight Rhoden and Alonzo King, providing models and clarifications of the concepts explored here.

Dance is thought made visible. –ALONZO KING, 1999

Uri Sands, the Impulse character, or the "hot center of the ballet," in Dwight Rhoden's *Verge*.

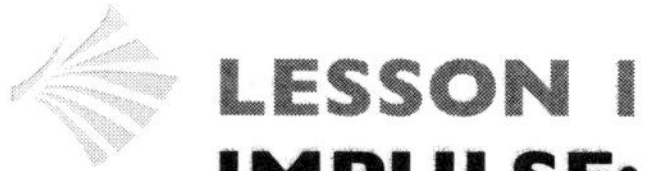

LESSON 1
IMPULSE: ORIGINS OF MOVEMENT

Introductory Statement

Movement is a neuromuscular event. In the body, the brain provides impulses to stimulate the nerves leading to muscles. The nerves elicit the desired muscular contractions that produce shapes and actions. Motivation (impulse) to move (action) usually comes from within. Dance is the interplay between impulse and action.

The concept of an impulse to move that begins as an idea in our minds and leads us into action is the main idea of the contemporary dance work *Verge* by Dwight Rhoden. He created a main character that he called the Impulse to personify the movement idea, or the catalyst for motion.

Vocabulary

abstract, abstraction
action
beginning shape
center of the body
choreographer
choreography
combination
flexion
focal point
impulse
isolation
range of motion
reaction
rotation
stimulus
succession
warm-up

Warm-Up and Impulse Discovery

- Explore movement successions through the spine, in the arms and legs, and from one body part to another.
  - **Example 1:** Begin lowering the head, followed by curving the chest forward, connecting to the waist while bending the knees so that you finish in a low curve, arms touching the floor. Reverse the succession to arrive standing upright.
  - **Example 2:** Starting with the arms resting at the sides of the body, rotate the right shoulder inward as you raise the arm upward, allow the elbow to point toward the ceiling, then lead the wrist upward, and finally the fingers, until the succession finishes with the fingers pointing toward the ceiling. Reverse this succession until the arm is once again at the side of the body. Try the other arm. Can you do a succession in both arms at the same time?
  - **Example 3:** Lift or point the leg to the front, rotate it inward and bend the knee, then bend the knee of the supporting leg until the two knees touch. Rotate the knee and leg outward and straighten the supporting leg until you undo the succession inward, and finish with the leg once again to the front.
- Create a series of body-part isolations focusing on just one joint and explore the movement potential and range of motion within this joint (for example, bend, stretch, rotate).
  - Begin by thinking about natural body operations such as breathing, hiccupping, or sneezing. Make a list of natural body actions and explore how they make your body move. Locate the center of the body weight (2 inches or 5 centimeters below the navel) and move from the center of the body so that the movement originates from the inside and escapes out to the extremities. Select eight different natural movements and give them a specific timing bookmarked by beginning and ending shapes. Simply do the natural motions.

- Make the natural actions into a new sequence and perform them one after the other. This time, alter each natural action in timing, shape, and size so it is no longer literal but starts to become a dance gesture. In dance, gestures are abstracted. The quality of the gesture rather than the literal gesture becomes important. Give each chosen action a new timing and order. Also use more than just the arms. Can some of the gestures be performed by the legs or head? Bookmark this new sequence with a beginning and ending neutral shape.

Sample sequence: Sneeze, hiccup, sigh, yawn, burp, breathe, sob, shudder.

Sometimes, the reaction to a stimulus originating outside the body produces an unplanned action within the body. The affected body part sends a sensation back to the brain, making the body respond unintentionally with movement to an outside stimulus rather than responding to the intent of the mind.

- React to imaginary stimuli from outside the body. The motivation to move comes from outside the body. Give the movements timing and beginning and ending shapes, and make them into a sequence.

Sample sequence: Bump into something, shoo away a fly, trip on your shoelace, dodge a punch, pet an animal, or react to a loud noise.

Structured Improvisations

EXAMPLE: Chapter 1, Lesson 1A: Defining an Impulse

In this excerpt from a teaching workshop, Alonzo King defines the concept of the impulse.

EXAMPLE: Chapter 1, Lesson 1B: Defining "Impulse"

In these four short excerpts, Dwight Rhoden is working with Uri Sands, the dancer personifying Impulse. Rhoden is helping Sands to understand the choreographer's concept for the central character and how he feels the dancer's movement should reflect this concept.

Improvisation 1: Points in Space

- Find four spots in four different locations in the room. Make sure these spots or focal points are clear and memorize the locations. The teacher will provide simple drum cues to stimulate the action, beating the drum and calling out the numbers "1 . . . 2 . . . 3 . . . 4," a number for each spot. First, simply turn your head toward each spot, focusing on the spot with the eyes at the drum cues. The teacher may call the spots out of order and in slow or fast time. Dancers may even call out the spots at random themselves. Next, point to each spot with the right index finger at the drum cues. Proceed to pointing with an elbow, then a knee, and finally with the whole body. Reorder the points at any time and change tempo to add interest. The sound of the drum and the chosen point in space are impulses motivating movement. The action defines the focal points in space while there is a reaction to sound cues.

• Turn and look at each spot because of an internal motivation such as looking for something, calling to someone, or waving hello. Develop a personal sequence of four spots that you have chosen because of specific motivations. Through movement, show the different reasons for focusing on each spot. There is no sound accompaniment. Note how the timing of the movement changes as your intent changes.

Improvisation 2: Isolating an Impulse

In this structured improvisation, an external action provides the motivation to move, or a reaction. Working in pairs, one partner closes the eyes and moves only when directed by the touch of the other partner. The active partner should touch a body part and the passive partner should move only the part touched. The passive partner should respond to the quality of the touch. If the quality of the touch is soft, the responding movement should be light; if the touch is forceful, the response should be strong. The active partner can also explore fast and slow touches. The passive partner is simply reacting to the impulse experienced and trying to isolate movement in the area touched.

Improvisation 3: Body Parts Take Control

Explore walking across the floor using a variety of levels. For example, take 4 steps with the knees bent, a low level; 4 steps on tiptoe, a high level; 4 steps in a natural walk; and finish with 4 natural steps, turning. Return across the floor dancing the same combination, but now lead the movement with your right elbow. The selected body part (the elbow) becomes the impulse that is motivating the rest of your body to move. Each time you start to move or change level or direction, the elbow must lead. Next try leading with your head, and then lead your movement with whatever body part you wish. Be sure to clearly emphasize the chosen body part that is working as the impulse for the movement.

Problem Solving

EXAMPLE: Chapter 1, Lesson 1C: "Impulse" Solo From *Verge*

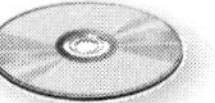

The solo is danced by Uri Sands. Watch how the choreographer uses natural gestures that have been given new timing and spatial configuration to make them into dance movement. There are arm, leg, and whole body gestures, some gestures literal and some abstract.

Impulse Dance

• Create an original Impulse dance that includes successions, focal points, isolations, action and reaction, and body-part leads. Begin with selected movements from the warm-up (successions, breathing, center-of-the-body impetus), and then work on focal points in space. Move on to movement motivated by imaginary outside touches, and finish with a sequence requiring a body part to lead the movement. There should be four sections to your dance. Determine an order, an appropriate movement for each section, and an amount of time (counts or phrases) for each section. The study should be 1 to 3 minutes long. See figure 1.1 for a sample Impulse dance.

• Perform your Impulse dances for each other. Audience members should watch to see how the impulses change and where they are coming from. Where does the movement start? Select music to accompany the finished study, or have a dance accompanist create a sound score. The teacher or accompanist may bring in music to assist the process.

Sample Impulse Dance

Beginning shape or stance
Succession sequence through the spine and arms
Snap, yawn, sneeze, sigh (with abstraction)
Body part leads to a new spot in the room
Quick shoulder and hip isolations, action and reaction
Sequence using imaginary touch
Focal-point sequence using head, knee, and foot
Body part leads to a new spot in the room
Ending shape or exit off

FIGURE 1.1 One example of an Impulse dance. In this lesson you create your own.

Discussion Questions

1. Define the word *impulse* as you perceive it.
2. Discuss the impulses in movement you observed in the solo from *Verge.*
3. Were movements clearly emanating from the center of the dancer's body?
4. Did you see any reactionary movement? If so, what was the character reacting to?
5. How did your own impulse solo show some of the same movement sources and action and reaction as seen in the *Verge* solo?
6. How did your intent and movement choices differ from those chosen by Rhoden?

Impulse: Origins of Movement

STATEMENT OF PERFORMANCE

Dancers will create an original Impulse dance that includes succession, isolations, focal points, body-part leads, and action and reaction.

Answer each of the following criteria with a yes or no and then score each category from 1 to 5, with 5 being the highest score and 1 the lowest. Use the rubrics to assist in discussion, self-reflection, and assessment of progress in understanding the choreographic concept. Students may grade themselves or each other. The teacher may use this as a guide for her own evaluation.

Criteria	Score	
CREATING: PERCEPTUAL SKILLS	YES	NO
The dancer did the following:		
1. Created at least four separate movement phrases based on abstraction of natural movement.	_____	_____
2. Used clear beginning and ending shapes.	_____	_____
3. Included successions, isolations, and body-part leads.	_____	_____
4. Gave a clear example of action and reaction.	_____	_____
Creating: Perceptual Skills Total	___________	
PERFORMING: TECHNICAL AND EXPRESSIVE SKILLS		
The dancer did the following:		
1. Remembered the choreographed sequence.	_____	_____
2. Clearly showed where the impulse started in each phrase.	_____	_____
3. Flowed easily from one action to another.	_____	_____
4. Retained concentration and intent while moving.	_____	_____
Performing: Technical and Expressive Skills Total	___________	
RESPONDING: INTELLECTUAL AND REFLECTIVE SKILLS		
The dancer did the following:		
1. Gave a purpose and rationale for movement choices.	_____	_____
2. Made informed critical observations of own work.	_____	_____
3. Made informed critical observations of the work of others.	_____	_____
Responding: Intellectual and Reflective Skills Total	___________	

SCORING

5 = Fulfilled all the criteria of creating, performing, and responding in a way that shows a thorough understanding of the skills and concepts to be mastered. Fully participated in the classroom tasks as a performer and as an audience member.

4 = Fulfilled all the criteria but does not yet show a thorough understanding of all skills and concepts. Fully participated in classroom tasks as a performer and as an audience member.

3 = Had difficulty fulfilling the criteria. Was not able to fully complete the assignment. Participated in class but could not complete all tasks as a performer and as an audience member.

2 = Did not complete the assigned work to a satisfactory degree. Did not fully participate as a performer or as an audience member.

1 = Did not participate.

ADDITIONAL COMMENTS

____

____

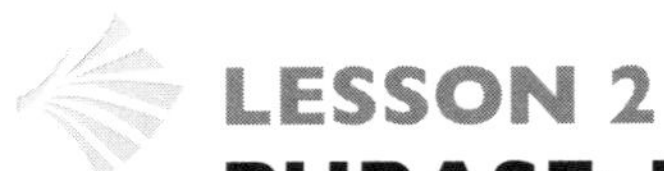

LESSON 2
PHRASE: LINKING MOVEMENTS

Vocabulary

action word
dance phrase
deconstruction
direct space
energy
flexible space
retrograde
sequence
space
time
transition

Alonzo King demonstrates a movement from a dance phrase to North Carolina Dance Theatre dancers Hernan Justo and Mia Cunningham.

Introductory Statement

In this lesson, the term *action word* refers to any word that motivates movement or defines body shape, such as *jump, turn, walk, run, asymmetrical shape, arabesque, isolation,* or *contraction.* Implicit in action words are the dance elements of time (fast to slow), space (flexible, i.e., curved and indirect, or direct, i.e., straight lines and angles), and energy (strong to light). Words that describe actions provide a base from which to create original dance phrases.

A dance phrase or sequence can be likened to a sentence formed when speaking. Sometimes we refer to dance phrases as *movement sequences.* For the purpose of this lesson either term is acceptable. Each phrase has a beginning, middle, and end. Movements selected in a dance phrase may flow one to the other naturally or may be connected by a transition movement. Evolving dance sequences from action words is another way to demystify the creative process. Action words lead to the formation of individual dance phrases and provide the framework for further developing those phrases into larger compositional forms. In this lesson, the action words are common terms used in contemporary dance.

Warm-Up and Action-Word Discovery

• Create a warm-up sequence that includes pliés, full-torso movements, leg swings, foot exercises, arm sequences, and small jumps. The warm-up can consist of movement from any style of dance. Name all movements and list them on a chart or blackboard. You may create new words for the actions or use familiar terms such as *knee bend* or *plié*.

• Make a list of favorite dance terms and movements, including those from the warm-up, and display the words on a wall chart or blackboard. Brainstorm to come up with as many terms and movements as possible.

• Select 10 words from the list that will become the foundation phrase for this lesson. Write each word on a separate piece of paper and post them in order on the wall.

Structured Improvisations

Improvisation 1: Words Become Action

• Create individual phrases based on the 10 action words you selected in the warm-up. All 10 words must be used. Make sure the transitions between words and their associated movements are smooth. Experiment with different levels, directions, and energy as you dance each word movement. Try to interpret each action word in several different ways. For instance does *roll* always mean to lie on the floor and roll like a log? What other ways can you roll? Make original interpretations for each word.

EXAMPLE: Chapter 1, Lesson 2A: Building a Phrase

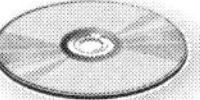

In this video excerpt Alonzo King introduces his thoughts about learning movement and then demonstrates his process for shaping dance phrases. Dancers from North Carolina Dance Theatre are challenged to interpret the actions that King gives them.

• Assign counts to the separate movements in the phrase so that the phrase is clear.

• Try performing the phrase twice from beginning to end. As you will see in the next improvisation, it is important to be able to repeat selected movement phrases so that you can play with the movement phrase.

Improvisation 2: Retrograde

EXAMPLE: Chapter 1, Lesson 2B: Can the Phrase Go Backward?

While creating the men's section from *Chants*, Alonzo King used the process of retrograde (doing a phrase in reverse order) to further develop his choreography. Watch how challenging this process was for the dancers to interpret but how interesting it was compositionally.

• Perform the phrase once more, but this time, start at the end and perform the phrase backward until you end in the beginning shape or move. Start from the end and go backward through all the words, using the individual cards to help. Post the retrograde version on the wall for reference. Discuss changes that might have to be made in the transitions between the different movements.

• Assign counts to this new phrase.

• Attach this phrase to the previous phrase you created in improvisation 1, Words Become Action.

• Try dancing the original phrase forward, followed immediately by its retrograde.

Improvisation 3: Deconstruction

• Take each of the selected action words from improvisation 1, Words Become Action, and write each one on a separate piece of paper. In a random fashion, perhaps by picking them out of a hat or drawing them like cards, make a new order for the phrase. Each word has a movement previously designed for it, but now each word has moved to another position in the phrase. By changing the movements around you have deconstructed the phrase and reordered it. Reordering features the same movements in a different and unexpected way.

• Discuss this process with classmates and the movement choices dancers made in order to reform the phrase.

Problem Solving

Following the Blueprint

• Create an original movement study from the three phrases generated in the previous exercises (see figure 1.2 for an example).

• Each study will include a core phrase (A), its retrograde (B), and its deconstruction (C). For example:

Core Phrase (A)	Retrograde (B)	Deconstructed (Reordered) (C)
Lunge	Balance on one leg	Hop
Roll	Leap	Lunge
Rise	Gallop	Balance on one leg
Symmetrical shape	Asymmetrical shape	Roll
Turn	Hop	Asymmetrical shape
Hop	Turn	Leap
Asymmetrical shape	Symmetrical shape	Rise
Gallop	Rise	Gallop
Leap	Roll	Turn
Balance on one leg	Lunge	Symmetrical shape

• Make sure the dance study has a clear beginning and ending shape or entrance and exit to and from the stage space.

• Select music for the study. The teacher or dance accompanist may offer suggestions and assistance.

• Perform your studies for your classmates. Audience members should provide feedback. Each dancer will have been working with the same words so the individual transitions and movement choices should be especially interesting to observe.

Two Blueprint Examples

1. The form of the study may be a rondo:

A core phrase
B retrograde
A core phrase
C deconstructed phrase
A core phrase

2. The form may be a theme and variations:

Original phrase (A)
Retrograde variation
Deconstructed variation
Original phrase (A)

FIGURE 1.2 Your movement study can either be in the form of a rondo or a theme and variations.

EXAMPLE: Chapter 1, Lesson 2C: Men's Dance From *Chants*

This selection features the men of North Carolina Dance Theatre in a group excerpt from *Chants*. The excerpt opens with an individual dancer presenting the movement phrase that will be developed throughout the section. He is followed by three dancers performing the same movement but reordered. The trio is followed by another soloist who performs the original movement phrase and inserts one or two new extensions to the movement material. Last, the group dances the phrase, with insertions, together.

Discussion Questions

1. How would you define a dance phrase? What does a series of movements need to have in order to be a phrase?
2. Is there a difference between a dance phrase and a movement sequence? Explain.
3. What other art forms create phrases?
4. What did you find challenging about composing a retrograde for a phrase?

Phrase: Linking Movements

STATEMENT OF PERFORMANCE

Dancers will create a study, Following the Blueprint, that consists of one 10-word phrase, its retrograde, and its deconstruction, and that follows one of the two suggested blueprints.

Answer each of the following criteria with a yes or no and then score each category from 1 to 5, with 5 being the highest score and 1 the lowest. Use the rubrics to assist in discussion, self-reflection, and assessment of progress in understanding the choreographic concept.

Criteria	**Score**	
CREATING: PERCEPTUAL SKILLS	YES	NO
The dancer did the following:		
1. Made good choices in timing and transitions.	_____	_____
2. Followed the assignment accurately.	_____	_____
3. Made a clear presentation of each action word.	_____	_____
4. Retrograded the phrase.	_____	_____
5. Successfully reordered known movements after trying out several different solutions.	_____	_____
Creating: Perceptual Skills Total ___________		
PERFORMING: TECHNICAL AND EXPRESSIVE SKILLS		
The dancer did the following:		
1. Accurately reproduced selected movement.	_____	_____
2. Demonstrated the correct movements for all phrases.	_____	_____
3. Flowed easily from one movement to another and from one phrase to another.	_____	_____
Performing: Technical and Expressive Skills Total ___________		
RESPONDING: INTELLECTUAL AND REFLECTIVE SKILLS		
The dancer did the following:		
1. Discussed choices.	_____	_____
2. Made informed critical observations of own work.	_____	_____
3. Made informed critical observations of the work of others.	_____	_____
Responding: Intellectual and Reflective Skills Total ___________		

SCORING

5 = Fulfilled all the criteria of creating, performing, and responding in a way that shows a thorough understanding of the skills and concepts to be mastered. Fully participated in the classroom tasks as a performer and as an audience member.

4 = Fulfilled all the criteria but does not yet show a thorough understanding of all skills and concepts. Fully participated in classroom tasks as a performer and as an audience member.

3 = Had difficulty fulfilling the criteria. Was not able to fully complete the assignment. Participated in class but could not complete all tasks as a performer and as an audience member.

2 = Did not complete the assigned work to a satisfactory degree. Did not fully participate as a performer or as an audience member.

1 = Did not participate.

ADDITIONAL COMMENTS

____

____

LESSON 3
GESTURE: PERSONAL VOCABULARY OF MOVEMENT

Introductory Statement

Gestures are movements that communicate meaning without using words. In dance, gestures are a rich source of movement material. In this lesson, gestures are first identified by their literal usage and then combined with the dance concepts of time, space, and energy to become dance movements. Each gesture will be experienced in different parts of the body until eventually they are transformed into dance movement. Gesture is transferred from simple arm, head, or shoulder movements to full-body actions.

Vocabulary

acceleration
deceleration
gesture
intent
mime
street dance
translation

© Rolland Elliott

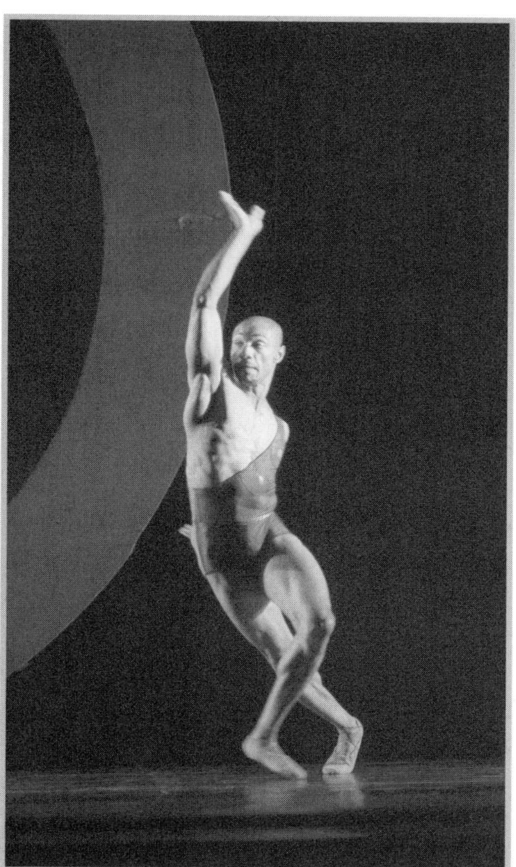

© Rolland Elliott

Uri Sands demonstrates two separate gestures from his Impulse solo in *Verge*.

Warm-Up and Gesture Discovery

- Explore a sequence of isolations in different body parts. Include movements from popular dance and move the isolations from one body part to another, such as those movements performed in the popular street dance move known as *poppin'.*

• Develop a sequence of simple gestures and perform them exactly as you might if no one were watching—in other words, normal usage. Here are some examples of gestures:

- Shrugging your shoulders
- Swatting a fly
- Covering your mouth during a yawn
- Pointing at a cloud formation
- Brushing hair from your brow

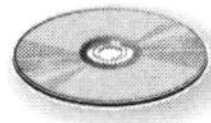

EXAMPLE: Chapter 1, Lesson 3A: Learning a Gesture Sequence

Dwight Rhoden is working with dancer Uri Sands to help him fully understand and clarify in time and space the gestures that motivate his solo in the ballet *Verge*. Each gesture is explained and given a specific motivation and timing. The final gesture in this excerpt is a stylized laugh.

Structured Improvisations

Improvisation 1: Gestures in Time

• Begin with the five gestures you practiced in the warm-up and come up with three more original gestures to make a phrase of eight common gestures (see figure 1.3). Make sure the whole sequence can be repeated. Use the natural timing for each gesture so that the phrase simply has a breath rhythm, or the natural rhythm of each gesture. Perhaps you might choose to associate a story with the gestures. The gestures should not be mimed actions, such as brushing your teeth or tying your shoes, but rather gestures used in real life such as waving, shaking hands, or shrugging shoulders.

• After performing each gesture in its natural time, explore individual gestures with different timing. For example, perform each gesture slower than normal, and then try doing each gesture faster than normal.

• Now perform the gesture sequence in strict 8-count timing, taking 1 count for each gesture. Repeat the sequence so that each gesture takes exactly the same amount of time to complete.

• Finally, take the 8-count sequence and perform it four times. Each repetition should be faster than the previous repetition in order to explore acceleration. The last repetition should be done as fast as you can.

• Perform the 8-count sequence four times once again. This time, however, begin quickly and gradually decelerate until the last repetition is performed extremely slowly.

• Discuss how the tempo change alters each gesture. Does the meaning of the gesture also change as the speed changes?

EXAMPLE: Chapter 1, Lesson 3B: Acceleration

Uri Sands performs the simple gestures introduced in the DVD example, chapter 1, lesson 3A, using acceleration to heighten the urgency of the moment. These gestures occur at the end of a solo in the ballet *Verge*. The acceleration of the gestures serves as a climax in the ballet.

Improvisation 2: Gestures in Space

• Use your original gestures or do the sample sequence suggested previously and alter the size of each gesture. Make some smaller, some larger. How does the size of the gesture alter its use of space? Exaggerate the pathways drawn in the air as each gesture is performed. Can any of the gestures be performed backward? As you discover new sizes and pathways for your gestures, how is the timing for each gesture changed? Perform each gesture as large as possible. Perform each gesture as small as possible. Vary the timing between gestures.

• Perform the sequence with new spatial variations in 8 counts, with 1 count for each gesture. How is the performance of the gesture altered because of the size change?

• Give each gesture new counts as needed. Because you have changed the size of the gestures, some may take more than 1 count to complete. Repeat the sequence with the new space-use and timing choices.

Sample Eight-Gesture Sequence

Neutral stance
Waving
Nodding yes
Pointing at something
Shrugging the shoulders
Scratching an itch
Shaking the head no
Covering the mouth while yawning
Pushing something away
Neutral stance

FIGURE 1.3 Take your original five gestures and add three more to create your own eight-gesture sequence.

Improvisation 3: Translating Gestures Into Movement

EXAMPLE: Chapter 1, Lesson 3C: Translating Gestures Into Movement

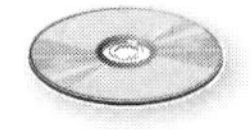

Dwight Rhoden describes to the dancers of North Carolina Dance Theatre how he interprets body gesture during a rehearsal of *Verge*.

Perform each gesture from improvisation 1, Gestures in Time, with a different body part. For example, instead of gesturing with the arms and hands, gesture with the legs or hips. How are the gestures different? Try performing each gesture with a variety of body parts.

Sample Phrase
Wave with a knee
Nod with a foot and hand
Shrug with the hips
Scratch your leg with the opposite foot or knee
Cover with an elbow
Push with the head

EXAMPLE: Chapter 1, Lesson 3D: Arms and Legs Together

Principal dancer Uri Sands dances an excerpt from *Verge* that demonstrates adding the gesture phrase to a simple walking phrase. Watch as Sands coordinates each gesture with a step.

• Begin by simply walking through the space. Each step should include one of the gestures from the Gestures in Time sequence from improvisation 1. Coordinate each gesture with a simple step forward, combining 1 step with 1 gesture using 8 counts. Combining your gestures with a step is not as easy as it seems and may require some practice.

• Next, repeat the sequence four times, gradually accelerating the walks. Perform the walking pattern, allowing each gesture with steps a different amount of time. Use the movements you developed in the final step of improvisation 2, Gestures in Space. The phrase will now take more than 8 counts. Discuss this process.

• Repeat the exercise using different locomotor movements with the gestures, such as jogging or jumping or a combination of both. Some gestures may work better with different kinds of movements, and you may choose to repeat them in your new phrase. Following is an example of a gesture phrase combined with locomotor movements. Counts are in parentheses.

Sample Phrase With Locomotor Movements

Run twice while waving your arms (1, 2).

Take one large lunge while slowly nodding your head (3, 4).

Step in four different directions while pointing the elbow in the direction of the step (5, 6, 7, 8).

Shrug your shoulders while jumping (1, 2).

Plié, rise to the toes, and plié again while slowly scratching an itch (3, 4, 5, 6).

Shake a leg (7, 8) while hopping.

Sink to the floor while covering your head with your arms (9, 10, 11, 12).

Problem Solving

EXAMPLE: Chapter 1, Lesson 3E: Translating Gestures Into Movement

Servy Gallardo performs a solo from *Verge* based on the gestures previously performed by Uri Sands. In Gallardo's solo the gestures are now varied and translated into full-body movement. Compare this sequence to the movement sequences discovered in improvisation 3, Translating Gestures Into Movement.

Body Gesture Study

• Create a 16-count phrase of arm movement only, which may include some of the previously explored gesture material and some new gestures. The phrase may have an underlying story, such as a conversation with a friend that escalates into an argument. Or, the phrase may simply be made up of random gestures, such as the gesture phrases developed by Dwight Rhoden.

• Translate each movement of the arms into a movement of the whole body or into another body part. Thus, the arms may originate a movement that serves to motivate new movement elsewhere in the body. The arm gesture may move from one body part to another in succession, or the whole body may create the arm gesture simultaneously. As the movement phrase develops, it will require new timing and counting.

• Repeat the original phrase with the arm gestures but add locomotor movement.

• As the phrases begin to develop, name the study. The study will develop like a theme with variations.

• Select music for the study (or the teacher may ask a musician to improvise with the performers).

Body Gesture Study

Beginning shape

Arm gesture phrase (A) (theme)

Translation of theme throughout the body and into space around the body (A^1) (variation 1)

Repeat of the phrase (A) (theme) with locomotor movement (A^2) (variation 2)

Repeat of the phrase (A) (theme)

Ending shape or exit

Creating the Scene

Perform individual Body Gesture studies consisting of the theme and variations 1 and 2. In these studies, each student has made individual choices about the initial arm-movement sequence and the translation of the arm gestures into the rest of the body and with locomotion. The process of creating the studies and the effect of the work on the audience should be discussed.

Discussion Questions

1. Define the word *gesture.*
2. How do gestures communicate to us?
3. Is gesture vocabulary the same across different cultures?
4. What common gestures do you use frequently? How did you learn them?
5. How did it feel to translate or develop a gesture from the arms to another body part?
6. Do gestures change their meaning when performed with different timings or in a different spatial configuration?
7. Does adding locomotion change the meaning of a gesture? Why or why not?

Gesture: Personal Vocabulary of Movement

STATEMENT OF PERFORMANCE

Each dancer will create a Body Gesture study consisting of an original arm phrase followed by two variations, one with translation of the arm gesture throughout the body and one moving in space.

Answer each of the following criteria with a yes or no and then score each category from 1 to 5, with 5 being the highest score and 1 the lowest. Use the rubrics to assist in discussion, self-reflection, and assessment of progress in understanding the choreographic concept.

Criteria	**Score** YES	NO
CREATING: PERCEPTUAL SKILLS The dancer did the following:		
1. Created a 16-count arm gesture sequence.	_____	_____
2. Included clear beginning and ending shapes.	_____	_____
3. Translated arm gesture to full-body movement.	_____	_____
4. Translated arm gesture to locomotion.	_____	_____
Creating: Perceptual Skills Total __________		
PERFORMING: TECHNICAL AND EXPRESSIVE SKILLS The dancer did the following:		
1. Accurately reproduced selected movement.	_____	_____
2. Created logical, well-crafted transitions between movements.	_____	_____
3. Counted each phrase and gesture so it was performed with music.	_____	_____
Performing: Technical and Expressive Skills Total __________		
RESPONDING: INTELLECTUAL AND REFLECTIVE SKILLS The dancer did the following:		
1. Discussed choices.	_____	_____
2. Made informed critical observations of own work.	_____	_____
3. Made informed critical observations of the work of others.	_____	_____
4. Noticed and discussed the similarities and differences among phrases.	_____	_____
Responding: Intellectual and Reflective Skills Total __________		

SCORING

5 = Fulfilled all the criteria of creating, performing, and responding in a way that shows a thorough understanding of the skills and concepts to be mastered. Fully participated in the classroom tasks as a performer and as an audience member.

4 = Fulfilled all the criteria but does not yet show a thorough understanding of all skills and concepts. Fully participated in classroom tasks as a performer and as an audience member.

3 = Had difficulty fulfilling the criteria. Was not able to fully complete the assignment. Participated in class but could not complete all tasks as a performer and as an audience member.

2 = Did not complete the assigned work to a satisfactory degree. Did not fully participate as a performer or as an audience member.

1 = Did not participate.

ADDITIONAL COMMENTS

____

____

LESSON 4
SHAPE: BODY DESIGN

Introductory Statement

Dancing can be thought of as painting in motion. The designs that moving bodies make in space provide viewers with aesthetic balance and form. Choreographers must place dancers in space just as painters must place forms on a canvas. The shaping of each dancer must constantly change as the dancer moves across the space. In this lesson, the concept of shapes made by the body is identified and explored.

Vocabulary

asymmetry
balance
levels
locomotor movement
nonlocomotor movement
shape (angled, carving, curved, spokelike, straight lines, twisted)
symmetry

Warm-Up and Shape Discovery

- Explore movement defined by the direction words used to describe the three spatial planes (vertical, or door, plane; sagittal, or wheel, plane; and transverse, or horizontal, plane). The central axes of these three planes cut through the body and define the three dimensions of our personal space. The vertical plane is defined by the words *rise* (up) and *fall* (down). The horizontal plane is defined by the words *open* (wide) and *close* (narrow). The sagittal plane is defined by the words *advance* (forward) and *retreat* (backward). The directions as defined by those three planes give points of reference.

Mia Cunningham in a middle-level asymmetrical shape from *Chants*.

© Jeff Cravotta

Jason Jacobs in a middle-level symmetrical shape from *Chants*.

• Freeze at various moments in the exercise and note the shapes made by the body. Explore movements based on the following shape words: angled, curved, straight, and twisted.

• Make carving movements in space. Make space around the body appear to move inward toward the body (curves) by gathering armfuls of air and bringing them into the body. Now try making spokelike movements that pierce through the space from the inside of the body outward (straight lines), pushing the air close to the body away from you.

• Explore rotation in different body parts that leads to twisted shapes. For example, what happens when you rotate your right shoulder down and forward? Explore rotating in the spine.

• Bend, extend, and rotate different parts of the body, and identify the resulting shape.

• Discuss the concepts of symmetry and asymmetry as they appear in geometrical shapes, in the body, and in groupings of people and objects. Improvise individual shapes that may be identified as angled, twisted, curved, or straight and as symmetrical or asymmetrical. Use all three levels (low, middle, and high).

EXAMPLE: Chapter 1, Lesson 4A: Shape Gallery

In this example, 10 shapes from the Impulse solo in *Verge* have been captured to provide examples of the shapes explored in the warm-up for shape discovery. Here are the shapes that Uri Sands demonstrates:

- High-level symmetry
- Middle-level symmetry
- Low-level symmetry
- High-level asymmetry
- Middle-level asymmetry
- Low-level asymmetry
- Straight shape
- Curved shape
- Angled shape
- Twisted shape

Structured Improvisations

Improvisation 1: Shape Sequence

• Create a shape sequence of six different shapes. You must include at least one shape that is angled, one that is curved, one that is twisted, and one that is straight. The other two shapes are entirely up to you. At least two of the shapes must be symmetrical. Make clear, planned transitions between each shape. At least one transition should be made with locomotor movement.

• Choose a partner and perform your individual shape sequences for each other.

• In stick figures, draw the shape solo you observed. Assist your partner in depicting your shape sequence on paper. See the sample shape score (figure 1.4).

• Exchange your shape score with a dancer from another pair so everyone will have a new score that is completely unfamiliar.

FIGURE 1.4 Sample shape score.

Improvisation 2: Interpreting the Score

Create a short shape study with original transitions that interprets the shapes drawn on the new score. The shapes may be interpreted in any way and on any level. Perform all the solos for each other and comment on original movement choices.

Problem Solving

EXAMPLE: Chapter 1, Lesson 4B: Shapes in Motion

In this section from his solo in *Verge*, Uri Sands demonstrates how the shapes introduced earlier are connected to become a dance. He demonstrates 12 different shapes that have varied levels, symmetry, and asymmetry and represent the shape characteristics of straight, curved, angled, and twisted.

Body Shaping Study

- Display all the individual shape scores on a wall. Choose two different scores of six shapes, each not interpreted in the previous exercises. Interpret the shapes from both scores to create a movement sequence motivated by shape. The shapes do not have to be performed in the sequence on the papers, but all 12 shapes must appear in the study.
- The Body Shaping study should include locomotor as well as nonlocomotor movement for transitions. Certain shapes may be repeated as needed as the study

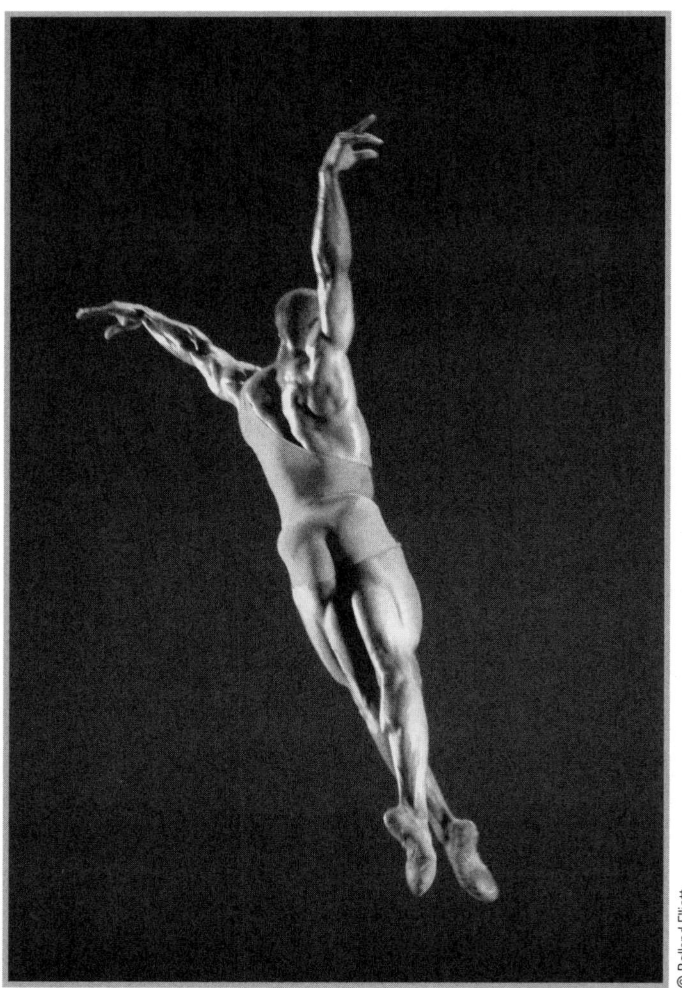

© Rolland Elliott

Uri Sands in a high-level straight shape from *Verge*.

progresses. The teacher will provide several selections of vocal sounds, or words only, to accompany the studies. Each dancer will find a title for the study motivated by the shapes.

Discussion Questions

1. Define the word *shape*.
2. In dance, how do we speak about body shapes? What are the different kinds of shapes our bodies can make?
3. Where do we start to make shapes in our bodies?
4. Discuss the concept of three-dimensionality. Name some three-dimensional shapes.
5. How do we achieve a sense of balance and proportion when making a shape?

Shape: Body Design

STATEMENT OF PERFORMANCE

Each dancer will create a Body Shaping study inspired by the shape scores designed by classmates.

Answer each of the following criteria with a yes or no and then score each category from 1 to 5, with 5 being the highest score and 1 the lowest. Use the rubrics to assist in discussion, self-reflection, and assessment of progress in understanding the choreographic concept.

Criteria	**Score**	
CREATING: PERCEPTUAL SKILLS	YES	NO
The dancer did the following:		
1. Included 12 shapes from two separate shape scores.	_____	_____
2. Had smooth, logical transitions between shapes.	_____	_____
3. Included symmetrical and asymmetrical shapes.	_____	_____
4. Had at least one locomotor transition.	_____	_____
Creating: Perceptual Skills Total	___________	
PERFORMING: TECHNICAL AND EXPRESSIVE SKILLS		
The dancer did the following:		
1. Accurately reproduced selected movement.	_____	_____
2. Remembered the sequence.	_____	_____
3. Performed an original interpretation of drawn shapes.	_____	_____
Performing: Technical and Expressive Skills Total	___________	
RESPONDING: INTELLECTUAL AND REFLECTIVE SKILLS		
The dancer did the following:		
1. Discussed choices.	_____	_____
2. Made informed critical observations of own work.	_____	_____
3. Made informed critical observations of the work of others.	_____	_____
Responding: Intellectual and Reflective Skills Total	___________	

SCORING

5 = Fulfilled all the criteria of creating, performing, and responding in a way that shows a thorough understanding of the skills and concepts to be mastered. Fully participated in the classroom tasks as a performer and as an audience member.

4 = Fulfilled all the criteria but does not yet show a thorough understanding of all skills and concepts. Fully participated in classroom tasks as a performer and as an audience member.

3 = Had difficulty fulfilling the criteria. Was not able to fully complete the assignment. Participated in class but could not complete all tasks as a performer and as an audience member.

2 = Did not complete the assigned work to a satisfactory degree. Did not fully participate as a performer or as an audience member.

1 = Did not participate.

ADDITIONAL COMMENTS

____

____

____

LESSON 5
PROBLEM SOLVING: CREATING A SOLO

Vocabulary

solo

Introductory Statement

In the previous four lessons, structured improvisations led to short movement studies that made use of the body as an expressive instrument for dance. In these lessons, moving from an inner impulse, building movement phrases from action words, identifying gestures and their meanings, and studying body shape were fully explored. For this lesson, dancers will pick one of the previously composed problem-solving studies for expansion into a 3- to 5-minute solo.

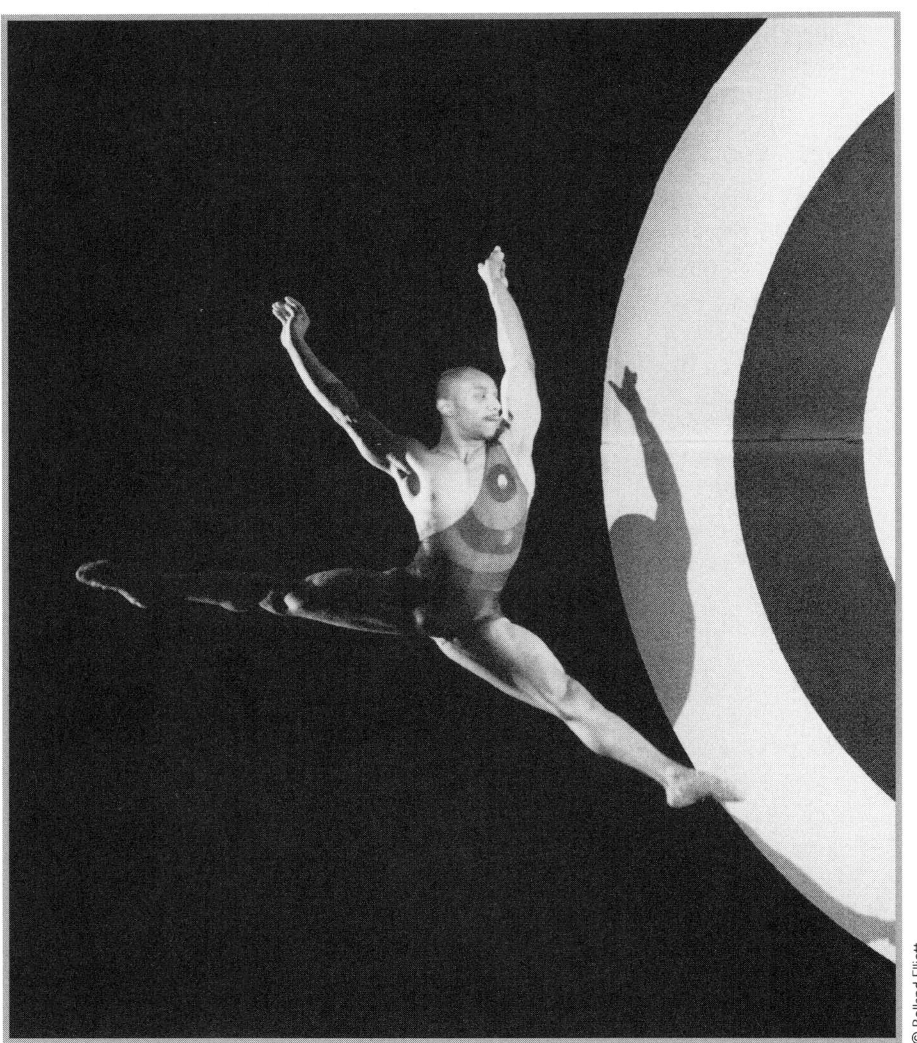

© Rolland Elliott

Uri Sands performs the opening solo from Dwight Rhoden's *Verge*.

Creating a Solo

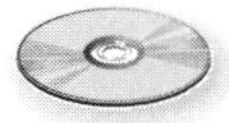

Choose one of the studies you have already created in class as a starting point for a solo. The already completed study should provide the beginning thematic material for the work. Create a solo that will incorporate information from the Impulse dance, Following the Blueprint study, Body Gesture study, or Body Shaping study. To begin, find a personal idea or theme for the solo inspired by the study that you have chosen to be the core of the composition, or take inspiration from the original works presented in the DVD examples provided in this chapter.

EXAMPLE: Chapter 1, Lesson 5A: "Impulse" Solo From *Verge*

Review this excerpt from the "Impulse" solo in *Verge* that you first watched during chapter 1, lesson 1, when the concept of impulses that generate movement was discussed.

Example 1

As a theme for *Verge,* Dwight Rhoden chose the idea of a character called "Impulse" who moves toward a goal. The goal is depicted as a huge target on the stage. The solo character personifying Impulse begins the ballet. In this solo, a series of gestures using clear straight lines depicts the direct line toward the target and the Impulse's desire to reach that target. The dancer and the target have a choreographic relationship to one another. The target is circular while the dancer is straight and angled; therefore, shape is immediately important in depicting the choreographic intent, along with the gestures designed to show the motivations of the Impulse. This solo incorporates the Body Gesture study, the Body Shaping study, and, of course, the Impulse study.

Example 2

In Alonzo King's *Chants,* the section called "Women of Butela" features a solo dancer dancing a series of movement phrases that correspond to the phrases in an African chant. Each movement phrase intertwines within the music phrase and appears to be improvised, although each phrase has been meticulously constructed. Watch how carefully the movement material is established and then deconstructed as each phrase is performed. This individual solo incorporates the Following the Blueprint and Body Shaping studies.

EXAMPLE: Chapter 1, Lesson 5B: "Women of Butela," a Solo From *Chants*

In this video example, the solo dancer, Anita Sun Pacylowski, holds the stage with individual dance phrases that intertwine with a solo female voice singing an African chant. Watch how the solo introduces the movement language and how each phrase relates to the other phrases in the solo. The corps of dancers on stage provides a simple movement backdrop to support the solo.

Discussion Questions

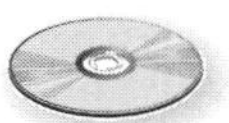

1. How might a choreographer take a phrase of movement material and expand it to become a finished solo?
2. What is the role of improvisation in generating material for a dance work? What is the role of improvisation in expanding established thematic material?
3. How does a choreographer decide on the formal structure for a dance solo?

Problem Solving: Creating a Solo

STATEMENT OF PERFORMANCE

Dancers will create and perform a solo based on the movement material explored in one of the four lessons in chapter 1.

Answer each of the following criteria with a yes or no and then score each category from 1 to 5, with 5 being the highest score and 1 the lowest. Use the rubrics to assist in discussion, self-reflection, and assessment of progress in understanding the choreographic concept.

Criteria	**Score**	
CREATING: PERCEPTUAL SKILLS	YES	NO
The dancer did the following:		
1. Selected and developed movement material generated from a previous lesson.	_____	_____
2. Selected an appropriate guiding idea.	_____	_____
3. Found original solutions to order movement material selected.	_____	_____
4. Clearly structured the solo with a beginning, middle, and end.	_____	_____
Creating: Perceptual Skills Total	_____	
PERFORMING: TECHNICAL AND EXPRESSIVE SKILLS		
The dancer did the following:		
1. Accurately reproduced selected movement.	_____	_____
2. Sustained movement intent and performance quality.	_____	_____
3. Performed movements that flowed easily from one to the next.	_____	_____
Performing: Technical and Expressive Skills Total	_____	
RESPONDING: INTELLECTUAL AND REFLECTIVE SKILLS		
The dancer did the following:		
1. Discussed choices.	_____	_____
2. Made informed critical observations of own work.	_____	_____
3. Made informed critical observations of the work of others.	_____	_____
Responding: Intellectual and Reflective Skills Total	_____	

SCORING

5 = Fulfilled all the criteria of creating, performing, and responding in a way that shows a thorough understanding of the skills and concepts to be mastered. Fully participated in the classroom tasks as a performer and as an audience member.

4 = Fulfilled all the criteria but does not yet show a thorough understanding of all skills and concepts. Fully participated in classroom tasks as a performer and as an audience member.

3 = Had difficulty fulfilling the criteria. Was not able to fully complete the assignment. Participated in class but could not complete all tasks as a performer and as an audience member.

2 = Did not complete the assigned work to a satisfactory degree. Did not fully participate as a performer or as an audience member.

1 = Did not participate.

ADDITIONAL COMMENTS

____

____

____

Student Self-Evaluation Questions

Name: ______________________ Date: ______________ Class: ______________

CREATIVE ASSIGNMENT

1. What was the most interesting aspect of what you did in class?

2. What was the most challenging problem you had to solve while you were working?

3. How did you try to solve the problem? Describe the process.

4. What did you learn while you were trying to solve the problem?

5. What was the role of improvisation in generating material for your study?

6. How did you decide on the structure for your dance?

7. What is another project or experience that might grow out of this one?

Chapter 2

Space: Exploring the Expanse We Move In

© Rolland Elliott

Uri Sands charts a pathway that culminates with jumping right to the center of the target in *Verge*. His pathway is straight and direct to hit his goal.

OVERVIEW

Space is the choreographer's canvas. The negative space on an empty stage becomes alive with movement as a dance work progresses. Choreographers must clearly define all the space use of their dancers by designing pathways on the floor and in the air, and they must fill the space with dancers making angles, curves, straight lines, and geometric figures with their bodies.

The general stage space (the space a dancer travels through with locomotion) and the dancers' personal space (the space that dancers can reach around the body with their limbs without moving both feet, using nonlocomotor movement) are terms used to categorize movement in space. Dance is a three-dimensional art form, so that rather than simply being a painter of space, a choreographer is also a sculptor. The dancer can appear to the audience not just in the flat front or back views but also obliquely, showing additional facings such as side, back, and diagonal views.

Most dance works are for an ensemble of dancers. The interplay of groupings, such as duets, trios, quartets, and full ensembles, provides unique challenges to a

Creation is principally the same for everybody. . . . You have an idea in your head like a blueprint, and you've seen a vision. . . . Your job is to reconstruct that vision . . . in the material world.

ALONZO KING, 1999

© Jeff Cravotta

Mia Cunningham in *Chants* moves in a forward pathway downstage while the other dancers move backward toward stage left.

choreographer. The interrelationships between the dancing bodies and their geometrical relationships and formations provide a visual balance and fill the stage with many shapes and figures for the visual pleasure of an audience.

In this chapter, we explore air and floor pathways in the stage space and the interpersonal spaces defined by dancers moving together. The choreographic problem of this chapter introduces the duet as a dance for two people occupying the stage space at the same time. Each dancer in the pair has unique spatial choices to make in order to balance the choices of the partner.

LESSON 1
AIR AND FLOOR PATHWAYS: MAPPING THE ROUTE

Introductory Statement

Dance pathways are of two kinds: air pathways and floor pathways. Air pathways describe shapes in space around the body and lead to the definition of body shapes. Awareness of the pathway of a gesture allows a dancer to achieve clarity in form and allows the audience to prepare for the ultimate shape that a dancer's body will assume. The floor pathway is the route along which a dancer travels through the general space of the stage. When driving on a trip we often need a map to help us find a route to take us from one city to another. In the same way, the dancer moves along a pathway to go from one designated point on the stage to another.

Both air and floor pathways have a beginning point and an ending point. If we begin and end at the same place, the pathway is called a *closed pathway.* If we end at a different place than that from which we began, the pathway is called an *open pathway.*

Vocabulary

air pathway
design
direct space
floor pathway
general space
geometric figures
interpersonal space
levels (high, middle, low)
mapping skills
pathway
personal space
zigzag

Definition of Warm-Up and Pathways

Air Pathway

- Explore movements that carve the space (curves and twists). Gather the space into the body. This use of space is called *flexible space,* that is, the space being moved through is rounded and indirect without an easily identified direction. Now explore making spokelike movements (straight lines) that move from the center of the body and pierce outward. Straight lines and angles are a direct use of space, that is, space is being cut through in a specific direction. Try making straight and curved lines on different levels: high, with the feet off the floor; middle, with the feet on the floor; and low, with some part of the torso touching the floor.

- Emphasize air pathways all around the body. Keeping the feet in one spot, use an imaginary paintbrush dipped in paint to draw pathways in the air that either carve or pierce the space. Print your name in the space around your body in very large letters. Write your name with cursive letters in the same way. Don't forget to write behind your body and use all levels. Paint curves, angles, and straight lines with movement all around your body.

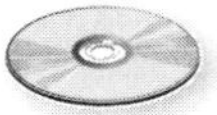

EXAMPLE: Chapter 2, Lesson 1A: Air Pathways

Dwight Rhoden works with dancers from North Carolina Dance Theatre in a beginning section from *Verge*. The section starts with the dancers describing air pathways in space while in silhouette, so all the dancers must be very clear about the size and timing of each pathway they describe. The dancers stay in one spot and describe the space around them with their arms and torsos.

Floor Pathway

- One way to understand floor pathways is to trace the route from one city to another on a map. Using a large map of the United States, identify the location of several cities such as New York, Miami, Chicago, San Francisco, Los Angeles, Dallas, St. Louis, Atlanta, and your home city. Place a pin on each of the selected cities. With crepe paper or yarn, draw the route to get directly from one city to another, such as the direct route from New York to Los Angeles. Attach the crepe paper of one color to the pins stationed at the end cities to delineate the direct, straight route. Try another two cities such as Miami and Chicago. Make sure the pathway between the two is as direct and straight as possible. All direct paths should use the same color of yarn or crepe paper.
- Map another route that may be indirect but more scenic. For instance, perhaps you might go from New York to Chicago by traveling around the Great Lakes. Notice how you could meander around each lake into Canada and back into the United States. You will eventually arrive at Chicago, but the route will be circular and indirect. Using a new color of crepe paper or yarn, pin the circuitous route on the map. You may need more than two pins at the beginning and ending cities. Each curve may need a pin. Try another two cities and draw an indirect scenic route. Use the same color of crepe paper or yarn for all indirect paths. Discuss the concepts of direct and indirect routes and use of space.
- Take the map off the wall and place it on the floor. Relate the map to the floor of a stage. You are standing in the center of the floor facing the audience. Imagine that north is upstage or behind you, south is downstage or in front of you, east is to your left, and west is to your right. You are inside the map, not looking at it. Make sure the map on the floor reflects the same directional orientation.
- Place yourself approximately where New York City might be and travel with a locomotor movement directly to the approximate location of Los Angeles. Note the pathway.
- Now try moving from Miami to Chicago. Use another type of locomotor movement. Perhaps you will go from Miami directly to Phoenix, Arizona, then to Chicago. The pathway now has an angle in it. Use a different locomotor movement for each leg of the journey.
- Place yourself in New York City again. This time take a tour of each of the Great Lakes. Go around each one into Canada, using a different kind of a locomotor movement to circle each lake. Finish your vacation in Chicago. Note the circular and curved pathway shapes you selected.

Structured Improvisations

Improvisation 1: Mapping the Floor

• Move along the floor while improvising simple walking patterns, such as a straight line, zigzag, circle, scallops, or any combination of these. The teacher or accompanist will provide percussion accompaniment and time the patterns to counts such as the following:

8 counts to zig, 4 counts to zag, 4 counts straight forward, repeat.

Walk 4 counts in a small circle, walk straight forward for 4 counts, walk to the right in 3 counts and clap, walk left for 3 counts and clap, walk straight backward for 4 counts.

• Vary locomotor movement choices for different parts of the pathways.

• Re-create one of the improvised pathways on a piece of paper. Don't forget to mark which direction is facing toward the audience. Imagine you are in the center of the paper. In front of you lies south, behind you is north, left is east, and right is west. Where will you choose to start? Refer to the sample stage (see figure 2.1).

Improvisation 2: Mapping for the Stage

Draw an original pathway on paper. The pathway should have a beginning point and an ending point and should include straight lines, curves, angles, and twists. Make the pathway cover the whole imaginary stage (see figure 2.2).

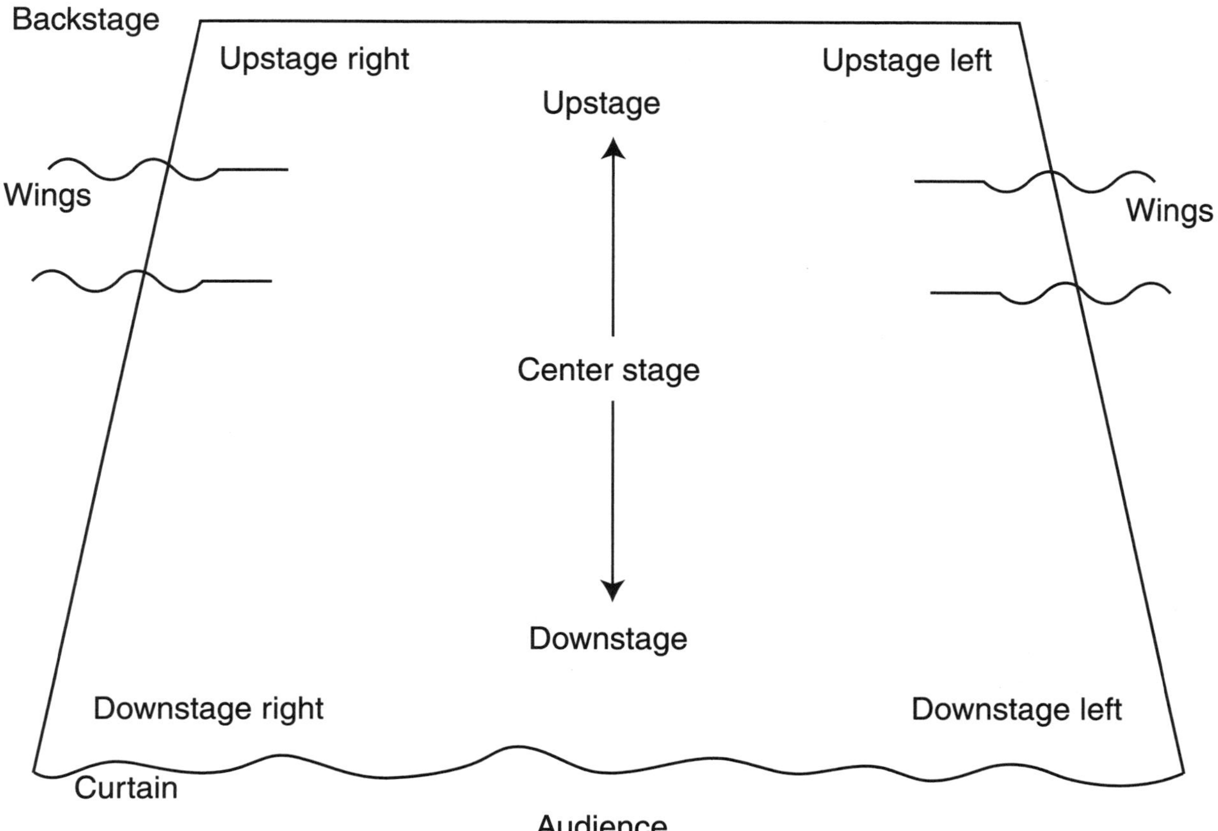

FIGURE 2.1 Sample stage.

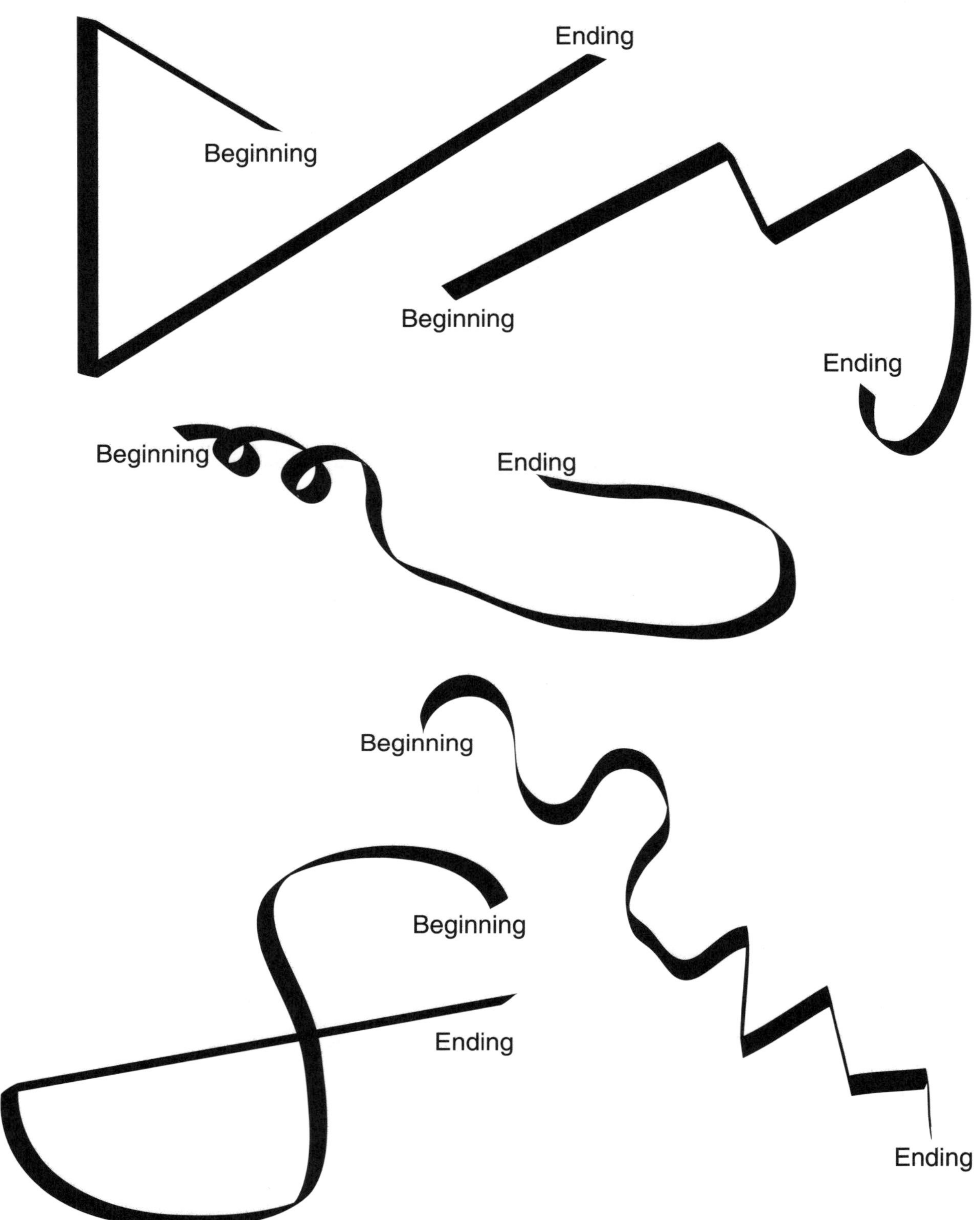

FIGURE 2.2 Pathway gallery.

EXAMPLE: Chapter 2, Lesson 1B: Air to Floor

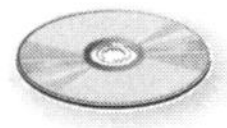

In this example, the dancers are combining a floor pathway with air pathways. They simply walk the path and then describe a shape in the body and in the air. Watch as the combination of pathways is masterfully modeled.

Improvisation 3: From Floor to Air

Exchange original pathway designs with other dancers and re-create a new pathway by drawing in the air with grand strokes around the body. Use a variety of body parts to describe different parts of the pathway, just make sure one foot stays firmly planted on the ground. Don't move in the space just yet; for now, simply translate the drawn pathways into body movement by drawing the paths in the air.

Improvisation 4: Pathway Dance

- Create original Air to Floor Pathway dances that include both kinds of pathways.
  - Design an air pathway with your arms that can translate into full-body movement following a predesigned pathway guide (A).
  - Translate the same air pathway to the floor with a variety of locomotor movements that cover the whole stage space (B).
  - Repeat the air pathway material with variation of timing or direction (A).
- Select musical accompaniment and give the phrases specific counts so that they may be repeated. The teacher or accompanist may make suggestions.
- Perform your Air to Floor Pathway dances for each other. Exchange observations with your classmates about the clarity and accuracy of the performances.

Problem Solving

EXAMPLE: Chapter 2, Lesson 1C: Groups in Space

Watch how Alonzo King uses varied floor patterns for the dancers in this group dance from *Chants*. In groups of four, the dancers follow carefully designed patterns in a square formation and along a diagonal. Note how the directness of the lines cuts through the space. The dancers move with little runs, big jumps, and turns of all kinds.

Dance Landscape

- With a partner or in a small group of three or four, look at several contemporary paintings depicting lines and curves on canvas that create spatial pathways. Suggested artists are Piet Mondrian, Jackson Pollock, and Wassily Kandinsky (see table 2.1). You can view paintings by these artists at www.soho-art.com. Select a painting that will become the inspiration for a dance. Notice the interweaving pathways depicted in the painting.
- Choose movement both in the air and on the floor that clearly describes all the different pathways that appear in the painting. Each dancer is responsible for creating both in the air and on the stage at least one pathway and, in some cases, more than one pathway. Because the painting contains all the lines and pathways at once, find a way for all the dancers in your group to perform the pathways at the same time. Make your pathways change levels at least once. Dancers may exit and enter at different times, or your group may choose to use

TABLE 2.1 Suggested Paintings

Jackson Pollock	Piet Mondrian	Wassily Kandinsky
Ocean Greyness, 1954	Composition No. 6, 1914	Tender Ascent, 1934
Gothic, 1944	Composition with Red and Blue, 1936	Upwards, 1929
Number 22, 1949	Broadway Boogie Woogie, 1942/43	*Sur Les Pointes*, 1928

chance methods such as throwing dice to determine the order of entrances. The stage space will be painted in movement traveled by all the dancers. Translate the painted pathways into original movement, re-creating the pathways depicted in the painting as closely as possible. The lines of the painting are the inspiration for the dance. Maintain an awareness of your fellow dancers even if you are not dancing together.

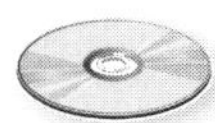

EXAMPLE: Chapter 2, Lesson 1D: Interweaving Patterns

In this section from *Chants,* we see the stage as we might see a painting. The stage space is painted with the movements of the dancers. Watch how each dancer or group of dancers enters and exits through the stage space seemingly unaware of each other but somehow belonging together. The scene is reminiscent of a watering hole on the African savanna in the early morning. The dancers enter the space with an individual dance phrase as if they were animals, a little wary of those around them and eager to leave as soon as a sip of water is taken.

Discussion Questions

1. How is the use of space different when moving with a straight line or a curved line? Which line might be described as flexible and why?
2. Can two or more people describe the same line in space? How might this be done?
3. Can we make an air pathway on different levels? Why might we want to do this?
4. How might we transfer an air pathway to a floor pathway? Are they the same? Explain.

Air and Floor Pathways: Mapping the Route

STATEMENT OF PERFORMANCE

A group of two to four dancers will create a dance landscape inspired by the pathways in a piece of artwork.

Answer each of the following criteria with a yes or no and then score each category from 1 to 5, with 5 being the highest score and 1 the lowest. Use the rubrics to assist in discussion, self-reflection, and assessment of progress in understanding the choreographic concept.

Criteria	**Score** YES	NO
CREATING: PERCEPTUAL SKILLS The dancer did the following:		
1. Included at least one air pathway.	____	____
2. Emphasized curves, straight lines, and angles in air and on floor.	____	____
3. Translated at least one floor pathway from artwork to floor.	____	____
4. Included at least one level change.	____	____
Creating: Perceptual Skills Total	________	
PERFORMING: TECHNICAL AND EXPRESSIVE SKILLS The dancer did the following:		
1. Accurately reproduced selected movement.	____	____
2. Made clear transitions from air to floor or floor to air.	____	____
3. Performed with an awareness of the other dancers even if not dancing together.	____	____
Performing: Technical and Expressive Skills Total	________	
RESPONDING: INTELLECTUAL AND REFLECTIVE SKILLS The dancer did the following:		
1. Discussed choices.	____	____
2. Made informed critical observations of own work.	____	____
3. Made informed critical observations of the work of others.	____	____
4. Noticed and discussed the similarities and differences among the studies.	____	____
Responding: Intellectual and Reflective Skills Total	________	

SCORING

5 = Fulfilled all the criteria of creating, performing, and responding in a way that shows a thorough understanding of the skills and concepts to be mastered. Fully participated in the classroom tasks as a performer and as an audience member.

4 = Fulfilled all the criteria but does not yet show a thorough understanding of all skills and concepts. Fully participated in classroom tasks as a performer and as an audience member.

3 = Had difficulty fulfilling the criteria. Was not able to fully complete the assignment. Participated in class but could not complete all tasks as a performer and as an audience member.

2 = Did not complete the assigned work to a satisfactory degree. Did not fully participate as a performer or as an audience member.

1 = Did not participate.

ADDITIONAL COMMENTS

____

____

____

LESSON 2
DIAGONALS: FROM CORNER TO CORNER

Vocabulary

corners
cube
diagonal
tessellation

Introductory Statement

To grasp the concept of the diagonal in movement, it is necessary to understand that three-dimensional forms are defined by height, width, and breadth, and that a diagonal is defined in relation to the three-dimensional solid of a cube with six sides and eight corners. Diagonals are oblique lines (lines that are neither perpendicular nor parallel) that are made by connecting the opposite corners of a cube, passing through the center.

Create your own cube from the tessellation provided with this lesson, figure 2.3, and identify the corners of the room and those of the cube. Imagine you are in the center of the cube.

Uri Sands and dancers in *Verge* create a large diagonal pathway across the space that extends from Sands' left fingertip high in the air to the opposite dancer's foot on the floor at the other side of the stage; from stage left high in the back corner cutting across to stage right low in the front corner.

In Rudolf Laban's analysis of movement called Labananalysis, the diagonals around the body afford the clearest three-dimensional use of the personal space around the body. The directions are identified by right or left side, high or low level, and front or back direction, so each diagonal has a label consisting of a side, level, and direction (three dimensions). Each diagonal makes an axis that cuts through the center of the body. There are four possible axes connecting the eight corners of the cube and crossing each other.

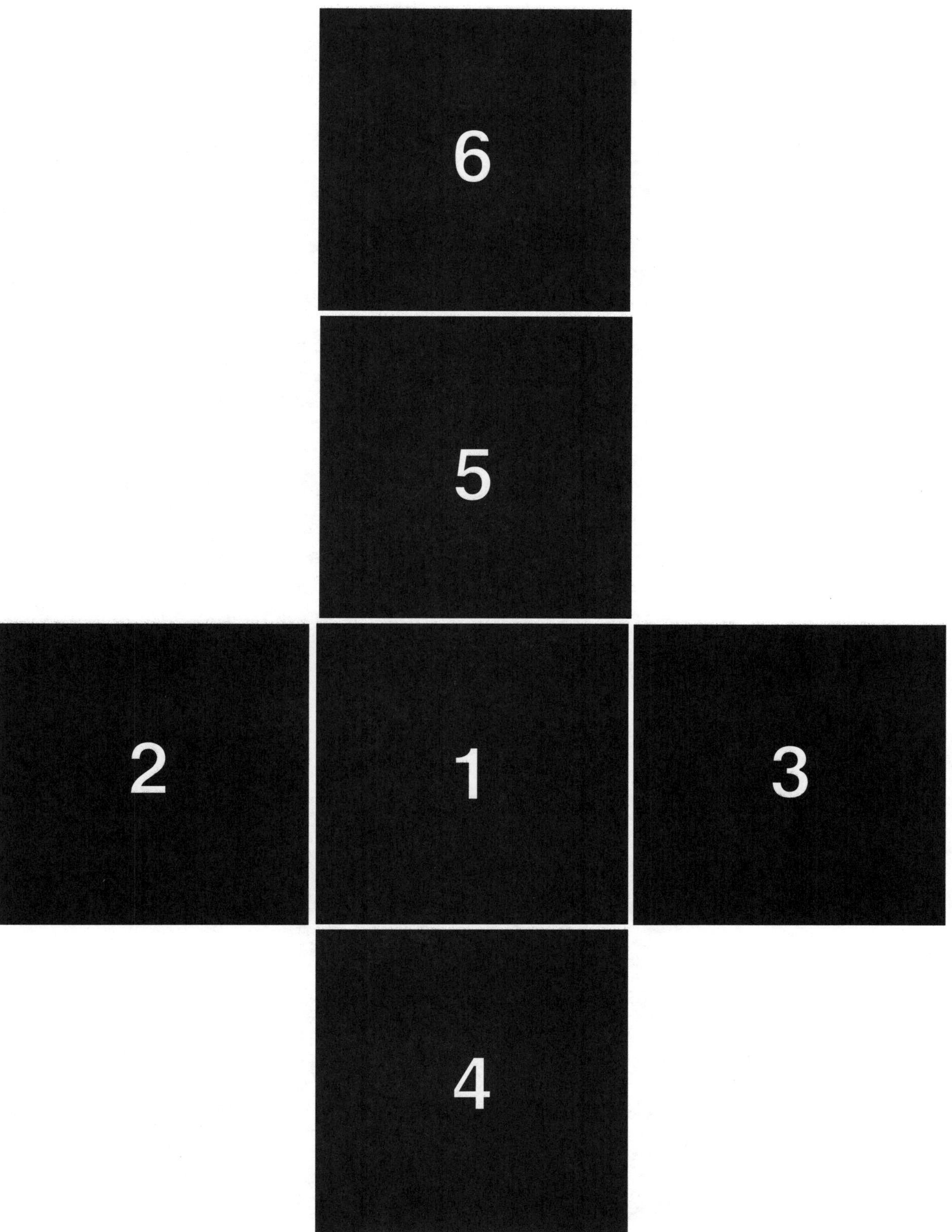

FIGURE 2.3 Tessellation of a cube. You can make your own cube using construction paper and tape. Photocopy the drawing onto construction paper, then cut and tape.

© Rolland Elliott

Dancer Uri Sands demonstrates reaching toward four corners in the room in a moment from *Verge*.

© Rolland Elliott

Dancers Nicholle-Rochelle and Heather Ferranti demonstrate a long diagonal from high back left (left arms) crossing the center of the body to low front right (left feet).

The four diagonals cutting through the center of the body in personal space are as follows: right high back to left low front; left high back to right low front; right low back to left high front; and left low back to right high front. The four diagonals use each of the eight corners as starting points.

In general space, the stage diagonals are made in floor pathways that are identified by the stage terms *upstage, downstage, right,* and *left.* The stage diagonals are as follows: upstage right to downstage left and upstage left to downstage right. The diagonal line as a pathway is the longest line in the stage space. See the diagonal lines on the sample stage drawing (figure 2.4).

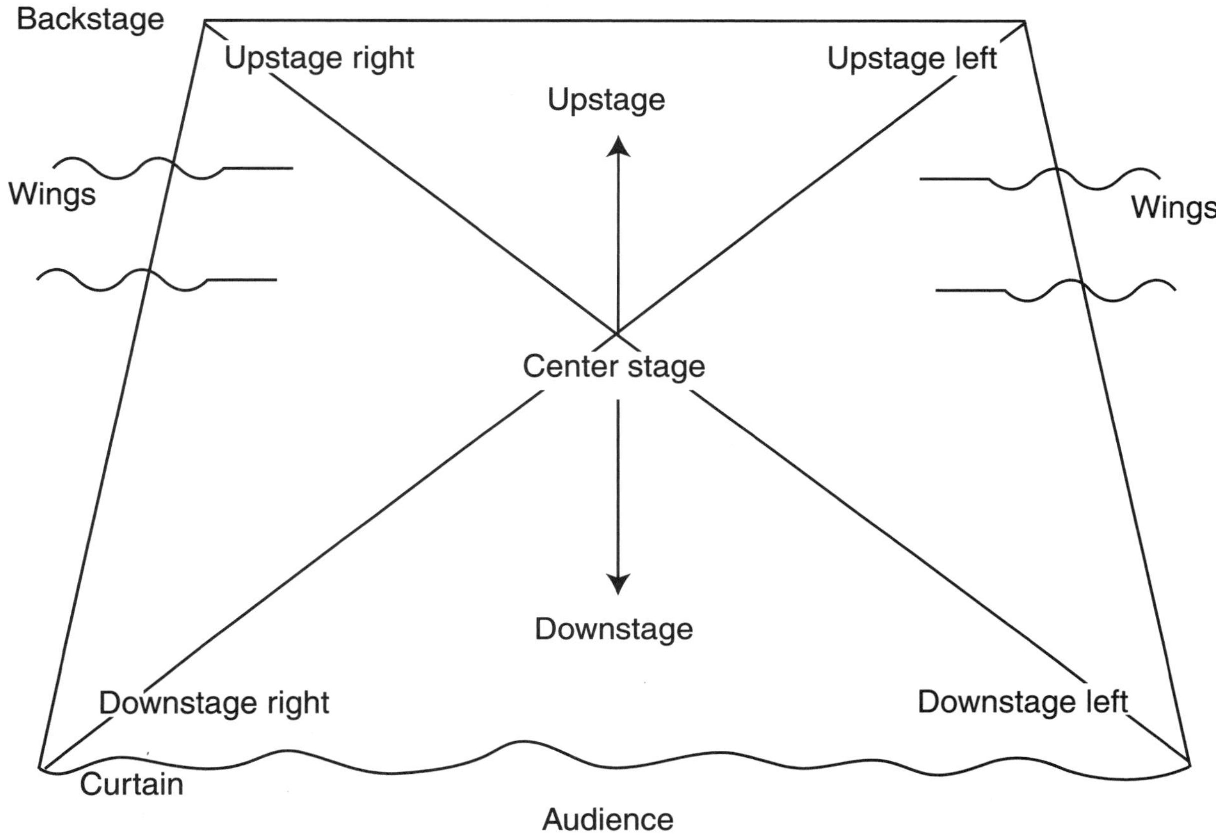

FIGURE 2.4 Diagonal stage lines.

Warm-Up: Personal Diagonals

• Review the warm-up from chapter 1, lesson 4, that explored movement defined by the direction words used to describe three of the spatial planes that cut through the body: rising to sinking (vertical plane), opening to closing (horizontal plane), and advancing and retreating (sagittal plane). Move into each direction in 8 counts, then try 4 counts. Vary the sequence, such as rise 4 counts, open 4 counts, then advance 4 counts, sink 4 counts, retreat 4 counts, and close 4 counts. Explore other orders and different counts.

• Reexamine the model of the cube shown in figure 2.3 (page 39) and relate it to the room. Count the eight corners of the cube and room. Label them as follows:

Right high back	Right high front
Right low back	Right low front
Left high back	Left high front
Left low back	Left low front

• Discuss the personal space around the body and identify the eight diagonal points in your own personal space, using direction, level, and side as if you were in your own cube. Relate personal space diagonals to the corners of the cube and room.

• Again using the tessellation model provided with the lesson (figure 2.3, page 39), use thread to connect the opposite corners of the cube, passing through the center each time. You have eight points and can make four diagonals throughout the space, cutting through the center:

1. Right high back to left low front
2. Left high back to right low front
3. Right low back to left high front
4. Left low back to right high front

EXAMPLE: Chapter 2, Lesson 2A: Diagonals in the Body

During a rehearsal of *Verge*, Dwight Rhoden clarifies the body shapes he wishes to see by emphasizing diagonal space. We see dancer Uri Sands not only making diagonal shapes in his body but also facing the upstage left corner and directing his diagonals to the downstage right corner. Thus, we view Sands "on the diagonal." We also see Dwight Rhoden working with the other dancers in *Verge* to clarify the top corner of his chosen diagonals.

Structured Improvisations

Improvisation 1: Stage Diagonals

• Stand in one corner and face the opposite one. Refer to the sample stage drawing with diagonals in figure 2.4 (page 41). The diagonals are as follows, going in either direction:

1. Upstage left to downstage right
2. Upstage right to downstage left

Because the floor below or wall in front is flat and two-dimensional, only two long diagonals are possible on the stage, running from one corner through the center of the room to the opposite corner (four corners, two diagonals).

• Move across the floor in pairs dancing a simple movement pattern such as four jumps and four runs. Now move across on the diagonal using a zigzag pathway. For each crossing of the room, use two different kinds of locomotor movement, such as a run on the zig and a hop forward on the zag.

• The teacher will distribute paper drawings of a stage. Draw the diagonals on the stage and label the starting points or corners. Identify and label each stage direction and the corners of the stage using both direction (upstage and downstage) and side (right or left).

EXAMPLE: Chapter 2, Lesson 2B: Diagonals on the Stage

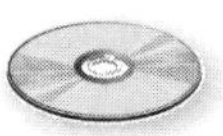

In this example, we see how Dwight Rhoden emphasizes the strength and power of the diagonal by creating movement that describes the stage diagonal beginning upstage right and moving downstage left. The camera was stationed at the downstage left corner to make the strength of the diagonal clearer.

Improvisation 2: Diagonal Shapes

- With a partner, select at least two loops of thick elastic or lycra material provided by the teacher. Together, improvise making diagonal shapes, using the elastic to emphasize each diagonal line. The elastic may be attached to your arms, legs, or torsos to delineate as many diagonals as can be found in each shape. The elastic may be used to emphasize the diagonal lines formed when your bodies make shapes together. Create with your partner a sequence of four diagonal pair shapes with smooth transitions between each shape manipulating the elastics as you transition between shapes.
- Share the shapes with classmates. Comment about the clarity of each diagonal. Often when working with elastic loops more than one diagonal in each shape becomes apparent.

Problem Solving

Diagonal Dance

- In partners, create original Diagonal dances that will explore diagonal space in shapes defining personal space (section A) and in general space pathways with locomotion (section B).
- Design a beginning shape with your partner, emphasizing diagonals. The elastic loops are optional at this point. Section A should include four nonlocomotor movement shapes with smooth logical transitions. Transition smoothly to section B. Section B should feature locomotor movement on different diagonals (zigzags) and move to a different spot in the room. Finish the dance in a diagonal pair shape.
- Perform the Diagonal dances in class with accompanying music or sound score as appropriate.

Discussion Questions

1. What are the names of the beginning and ending points of the two long diagonals that can be drawn on the stage floor?
2. What are the names of the eight end points of the four diagonals we can draw around the body in our personal space?
3. Do we use diagonals when we are mapping routes for a trip? How and why?
4. Can we walk a diagonal with different body facings? How?
5. Why would we want to use diagonal space in choreographing a dance?

Diagonals: From Corner to Corner

STATEMENT OF PERFORMANCE

In duets, dancers will create an original Diagonal dance.

Answer each of the following criteria with a yes or no and then score each category from 1 to 5, with 5 being the highest score and 1 the lowest. Use the rubrics to assist in discussion, self-reflection, and assessment of progress in understanding the choreographic concept.

Criteria	**Score**	
CREATING: PERCEPTUAL SKILLS	YES	NO
The dancers did the following:		
1. Created four nonlocomotor pair shapes (section A) using diagonals describing personal space.	_____	_____
2. Transitioned smoothly and logically between shapes.	_____	_____
3. Included an ending shape with clear diagonals.	_____	_____
4. Performed locomotor movement sequences along selected stage diagonals (section B).	_____	_____
Creating: Perceptual Skills Total	__________	
PERFORMING: TECHNICAL AND EXPRESSIVE SKILLS		
The dancers did the following:		
1. Accurately reproduced selected movement.	_____	_____
2. Transitioned easily between section A and section B.	_____	_____
3. Retained strong directional focus throughout the performance.	_____	_____
4. Performed successfully and reliably with a partner.	_____	_____
Performing: Technical and Expressive Skills Total	__________	
RESPONDING: INTELLECTUAL AND REFLECTIVE SKILLS		
The dancers did the following:		
1. Discussed choices.	_____	_____
2. Made informed critical observations of own work.	_____	_____
3. Made informed critical observations of the work of others.	_____	_____
4. Noticed and discussed the similarities and differences of own work in comparison with the work of others.	_____	_____
Responding: Intellectual and Reflective Skills Total	__________	

SCORING

5 = Fulfilled all the criteria of creating, performing, and responding in a way that shows a thorough understanding of the skills and concepts to be mastered. Fully participated in the classroom tasks as a performer and as an audience member.

4 = Fulfilled all the criteria but does not yet show a thorough understanding of all skills and concepts. Fully participated in classroom tasks as a performer and as an audience member.

3 = Had difficulty fulfilling the criteria. Was not able to fully complete the assignment. Participated in class but could not complete all tasks as a performer and as an audience member.

2 = Did not complete the assigned work to a satisfactory degree. Did not fully participate as a performer or as an audience member.

1 = Did not participate.

ADDITIONAL COMMENTS

____

____

LESSON 3
SYMMETRY: BALANCING SHAPES

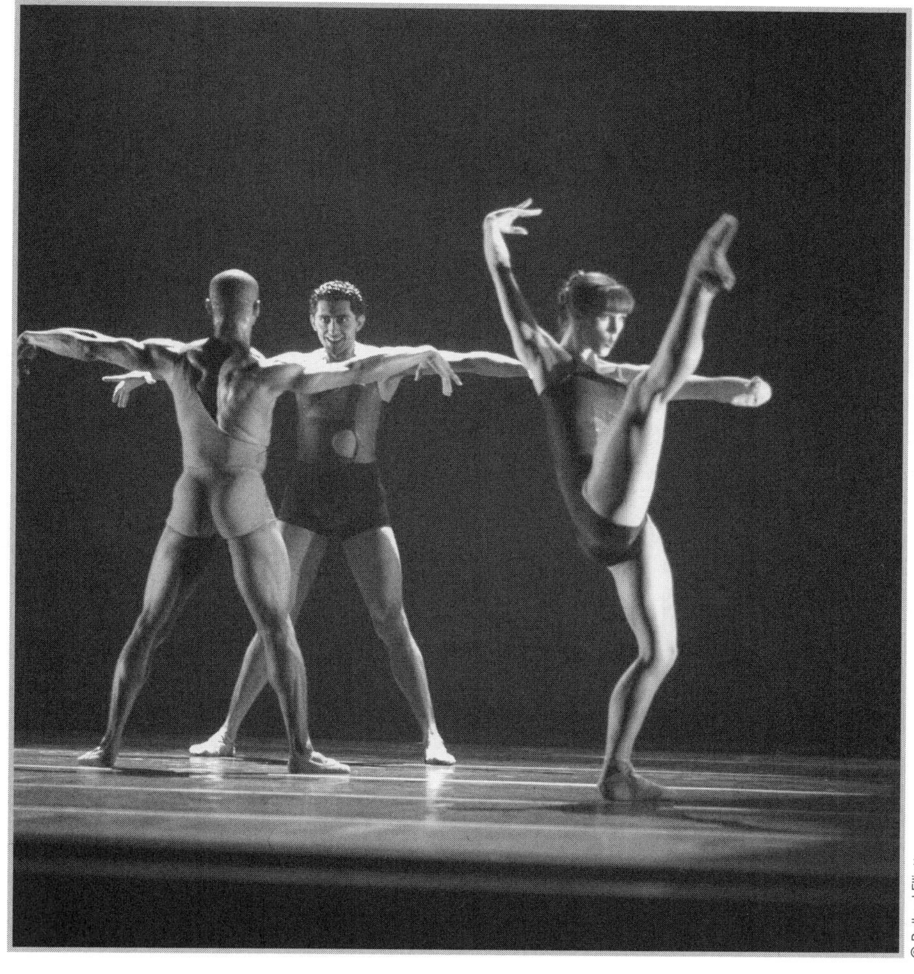

© Rolland Elliott

Uri Sands and Edgar Vardanian dance a mirroring sequence in the center of the stage while Nicholle-Rochelle dances a solo around them in this section from *Verge*.

Vocabulary

asymmetry
balance
interpersonal space
mirroring
reflection
reflection line
reverse
symmetry
visual balance

Introductory Statement

To reflect an object in dance means to produce its mirror image in relationship to a reflecting line that divides the space into two parts. On the stage, the reflection line may divide the space horizontally, creating an upstage side and a downstage side, or vertically, creating a stage-left side and a stage-right side.

Dance movements producing a reflection are called mirroring movements. While mirroring, each dancer or group of dancers claims one side of the divided space. In *literal mirroring,* a term coined for these lessons, dancers always dance the same movements, as if looking at each other in a mirror. In this case, the dancers face one another with one dancer following the lead of the other using opposite limbs or sides of the body (e.g., dancer A curves to her left; dancer B mirrors by curving his body to his right). Dancers move in exactly the same way and at the same time, as if only one person were moving. When dancers move both sides of their bodies together to create symmetrical shapes, they balance each other in space and produce visual symmetry. If they choose to move only one side of the body, the audience will see asymmetry because the body shape of both dancers is delineated on one side of the body only.

Dancers facing each other may also create *lateral mirroring,* another term coined for these lessons. In this case, each dancer does the same movement as the partner but uses the same arms and legs (e.g., dancer A curves to her right; dancer B curves to his right). When the dancers move the same side of the body, the audience will see a balanced, symmetrical shape made out of the two sides of the mirror figure. Each dancer becomes one side of the observed shape. In this kind of mirroring, symmetry is always observed.

Both types of mirroring provide a satisfying visual balance and use of space. Observers become aware of the concept of interpersonal space, or the space and spatial relationships activated between two or more people. In this lesson, dancers will explore literal as well as lateral mirroring.

Warm-Up: Mirroring

- Select one dancer as leader to improvise a literal mirroring warm-up that may include material from the previous lessons: successions, isolations, body-part leading, and inward and outward rotation with gestures. The other dancers or followers should try to mirror the leader in terms of time, space, and energy. Music to complement the exercise should be in a tempo that will allow maximum dancer focus on the selected movements.
- In pairs, explore literal mirroring with one leader and one follower. Dancers remain in one place but vary levels and speeds and find several still shapes. Music to accompany the exercise should now be varied. Try the improvisation with four different types of music. Both partner A and partner B should have a chance to lead.

Structured Improvisations

Improvisation 1: Drawing a Mirrored Shape

- Study the sample graph reflection (see figure 2.5). Take a piece of graph paper, a pencil, and a ruler and draw a reflecting line down the center of the paper vertically. Draw a geometric figure on one side of the line and then draw its exact reflection on the other side using line segments, points, perpendicular lines, parallel lines, and diagonals. Study the symmetry of the figures. Turn the paper so that the reflecting line is horizontal. Compare how the figure looks from this vantage point with the original facing.
- Share your graphs with the rest of the class. How might mirrored movement phrases be perceived by an audience? How do we as dancers perceive symmetry while moving? What makes something symmetrical?

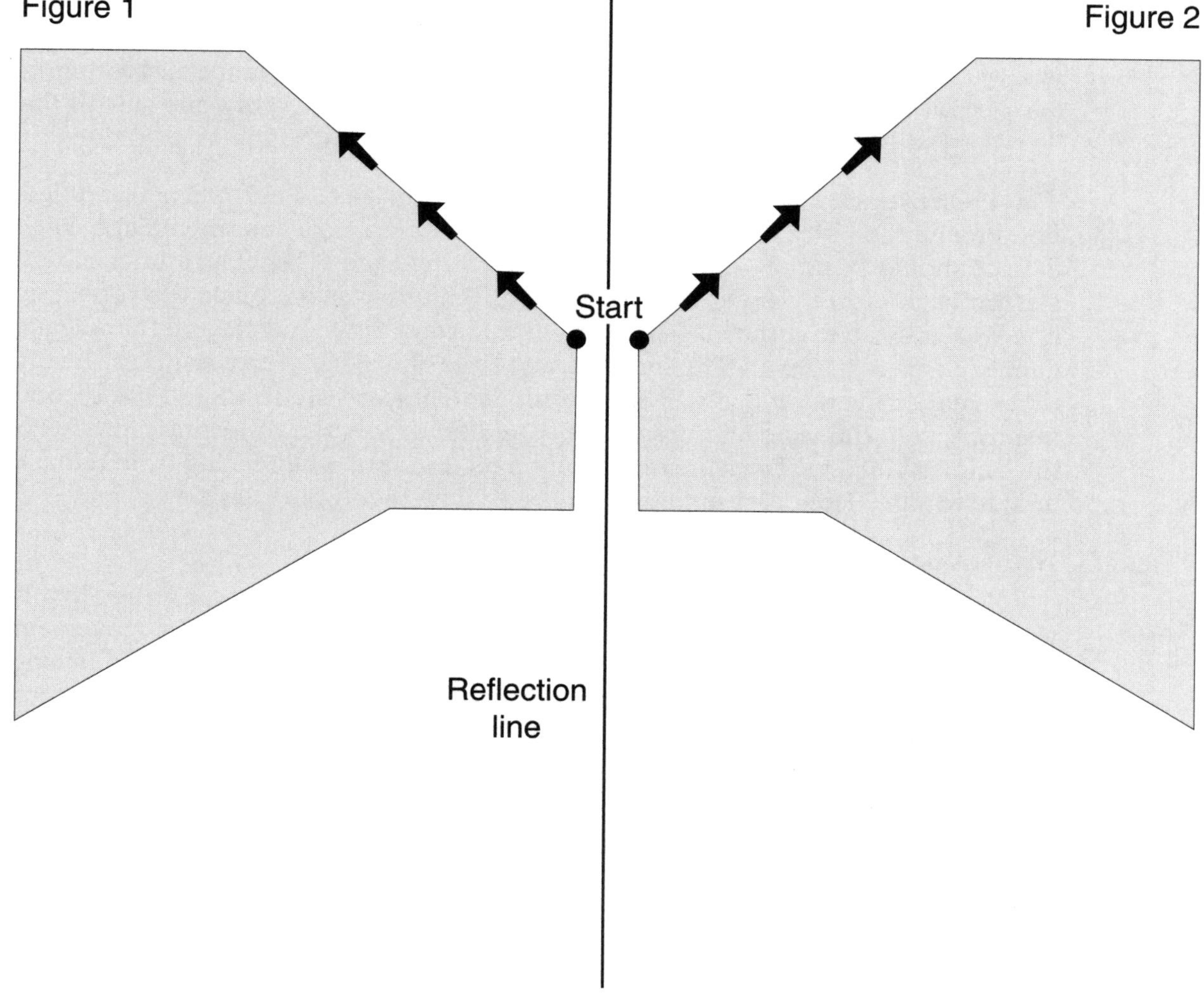

FIGURE 2.5 Sample graph reflection.

Improvisation 2: Reflection Sequence

- Individually, develop a 16-count sequence of movement that uses material from a previous lesson. For example, the gesture sequence from chapter 1, lesson 3, would be fun to use. Find your mirroring partner. Teach each other the 16-count phrases so that when finished, each pair has a 32-count phrase (16 counts from each partner). Partners should begin with the same arm and leg so that they are always using the same side of the body. Practice the 32-count phrase to make sure both dancers can perform it from memory.
- Face each other and perform the 32-count sequence in a lateral mirroring fashion. Both partners will perform the phrase as they learned it, starting on the same side of the body. This time the movement will seem different because the partners are now facing each other. Symmetry is produced because movement on both sides of the figure is seen simultaneously when viewed front to back. Discuss the ease or difficulty of this exercise.

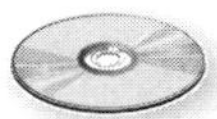

EXAMPLE: Chapter 2, Lesson 3A: Mirroring

In *Verge*, Dwight Rhoden created two lead characters: the Impulse, whom we met in chapter 1, and the Alter Ego. In this example the Impulse and the Alter Ego demonstrate lateral mirroring. The dancers are doing the same movement facing each other but are using the same arms and legs so that the shapes they make in space are symmetrical. Note the small and full body gestures.

- Present each lateral mirroring sequence to the class. First, place the reflection line horizontally, dividing the stage space into upstage and downstage. Each dancer should stand on one side of the line facing each other. The audience will see the back of one dancer and the front of the other. Next, place the reflecting line vertically so that the stage is divided into stage right and stage left and each dancer faces a side wall The audience will see the sides of the dancers. In the first instance the audience will see the movement from the front and the second instance from the side. Discuss with the audience how the reflections look with the different facings. Does the movement look different when facing front to back or side to side? How is symmetry achieved when facing sideways?

Improvisation 3: Looking in the Mirror

- Create a variation of the lateral mirroring sequence with literal mirroring. In this variation, both partners will use the same arms and legs while doing the movement phrase facing each other (horizontal reflection line). The dancer who is following will have to reverse beginning sides when starting each movement. Practice your 32-count sequence from the lateral mirroring exercise in this manner. Each partner must do the movement with the opposite arm and leg. This process will produce spatial asymmetry because only one side of a figure in space will be observed.
- Present each literal mirroring sequence to the class. Next, place the reflecting line vertically so that each dancer faces a side wall. Dance the same literal mirroring movements just danced with the horizontal reflecting line. In the first instance the audience saw the movement from the front, in the second instance from the side. Discuss how the reflections look with the different facings. Does the movement look different when facing front to back or side to side? How is symmetry achieved when facing sideways?

Improvisation 4: Side by Side

Using the same 32-count movement phrase created for improvisation 3, dance it standing side by side, both dancers facing the audience or front. To achieve symmetry, each dancer must begin with the opposite side or limbs of the body. The reflection line is vertical, dividing the stage in two halves, left and right. In this relationship, the dancer on stage left will begin with the left foot and the dancer on stage right will begin with the right foot. Is it easier or harder to remain in unison? How does this exercise relate to the graphed forms drawn earlier?

EXAMPLE: Chapter 2, Lesson 3B: Opening and Closing Duet

Alonzo King uses the compositional device of mirroring in his work *Dreamer.* In this example, we can see lateral mirroring front to back, side by side, and back to back. The reflection line is always horizontal, however. Watch how the relationship between dancers evolves as facings change.

Improvisation 5: Back to Back

- Using the same 32-count movement phrase previously explored, dance it while standing back to back. First, perform it as a literal mirroring sequence using the opposite arms and legs, then try a lateral mirroring sequence using same arms and legs. Perform your sequences for the class. Place the reflection line horizontally, dividing the stage into upstage and downstage halves. One dancer will face the front, the other will face the back wall. Discuss with classmates which of the two types of mirroring, literal or lateral, is most interesting visually. How might a choreographer use this type of back-to-back mirroring?

EXAMPLE: Chapter 2, Lesson 3C: Back to Back

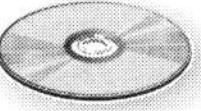

In this example from *Verge*, watch the two dancers in the center dance the same movement with the same arms and legs but starting back to back. The reflection line is horizontal and the dancers face away from each other. This relationship gives the illusion that the dancers are moving away from and toward the center of the stage. One dancer moves toward the audience as the other moves away.

- Perform the different mirroring variations from improvisations 2 through 5. Each pair should choose one or more of the variations to perform. With your partner, decide how to place the reflection line to divide the stage. Discuss with classmates which of the mirroring variations is most interesting and why.

Problem Solving

EXAMPLE: Chapter 2, Lesson 3D: At the Bull's-Eye

In *Verge*, the Alter Ego mimics the movements of the Impulse, especially as he enters the center of the target. In this example, we see both characters performing a mirroring sequence that begins with symmetrical arm, leg, and body movement followed by literal and lateral mirroring gestures. The stage is bisected by a horizontal reflection line so that we see one dancer from the back and the other from the front. They are standing as if looking in a mirror.

Reflection Duets

- In partners, design a Reflection duet inspired by the movement material explored in improvisations 2 through 5, which can serve as a starting point for a new series of 32 counts.
- Design the sequence using literal mirroring (section A). Repeat the sequence using lateral mirroring (section B). Perform the phrase a third time, mixing and matching literal and lateral mirroring (section C). Try the sequences facing each other, back to back, or side by side. Decide which facing is appropriate for each sequence. Also decide where the reflection line should be for each group of 32 counts so that the material will appear the most interesting to the audience. At least one section should show the stage space divided horizontally, one vertically, and one a combination of the two. The study should be at least 1 minute long.

Sample Phrase

A = Literal mirroring, 32 counts, horizontal reflection line, dancers are face to face

B = Lateral mirroring, 32 counts, vertical reflection line, dancers are face to face

C = Lateral mirroring back to back and side to side, 32 counts, horizontal reflection line

Discussion Questions

1. When we look in a mirror, do we see ourselves as others see us or are we reversed?
2. To mirror someone, what must we do?
3. What happens when mirroring partners do the same movement starting with the same-side arms and legs? How is this different from traditional mirroring?
4. Are some kinds of movements easier or harder to do with a mirroring partner?
5. Is it possible to make mirroring shapes?
6. How is symmetry achieved in mirroring?

Symmetry: Balancing Shapes

STATEMENT OF PERFORMANCE

In partners, dancers will create a Reflection duet of approximately 1 minute in length that includes literal mirroring face to face, lateral mirroring, back-to-back and side-by-side facings, and changing reflection lines (vertical and horizontal).

Answer each of the following criteria with a yes or no and then score each category from 1 to 5, with 5 being the highest score and 1 the lowest. Use the rubrics to assist in discussion, self-reflection, and assessment of progress in understanding the choreographic concept.

Criteria	**Score**	
CREATING: PERCEPTUAL SKILLS	YES	NO
The dancer did the following:		
1. Made a 32-count phrase performed with literal mirroring.	_____	_____
2. Made a 32-count variation performed with lateral mirroring.	_____	_____
3. Created a third repetition of the phrase using both literal and lateral mirroring.	_____	_____
4. Used both vertical and horizontal reflection lines.	_____	_____
5. Incorporated back-to-back and side-by-side spatial orientations.	_____	_____
Creating: Perceptual Skills Total	___________	
PERFORMING: TECHNICAL AND EXPRESSIVE SKILLS		
The dancer did the following:		
1. Accurately reproduced selected movement.	_____	_____
2. Performed the three phrases with smooth transitions between each.	_____	_____
3. Repeated chosen phrases with new facings.	_____	_____
Performing: Technical and Expressive Skills Total	___________	
RESPONDING: INTELLECTUAL AND REFLECTIVE SKILLS		
The dancer did the following:		
1. Discussed choices.	_____	_____
2. Made informed critical observations of own work.	_____	_____
3. Made informed critical observations of the work of others.	_____	_____
4. Noticed and discussed the similarities and differences between groups.	_____	_____
Responding: Intellectual and Reflective Skills Total	___________	

SCORING

5 = Fulfilled all the criteria of creating, performing, and responding in a way that shows a thorough understanding of the skills and concepts to be mastered. Fully participated in the classroom tasks as a performer and as an audience member.

4 = Fulfilled all the criteria but does not yet show a thorough understanding of all skills and concepts. Fully participated in classroom tasks as a performer and as an audience member.

3 = Had difficulty fulfilling the criteria. Was not able to fully complete the assignment. Participated in class but could not complete all tasks as a performer and as an audience member.

2 = Did not complete the assigned work to a satisfactory degree. Did not fully participate as a performer or as an audience member.

1 = Did not participate.

ADDITIONAL COMMENTS

____

____

LESSON 4
POSITIVE AND NEGATIVE SPACE: SHARING A SHAPE

Vocabulary

asymmetry
balance
interlocking forms
levels
negative space
pas de deux
positive space
shape

Introductory Statement

Interlocking forms and shapes created by two dancers occur frequently in dance. In a duet (called *pas de deux* in ballet), two dancers dance together using locomotor and nonlocomotor movement leading to moments of shared shapes to express choreographic intent. All of the shapes must be balanced visually and consist of the same kinds of shapes identified in chapter 1, lesson 4 (angled, curved, straight lines, twisted). When watching a duet, we see shape after shape made by the two dancers. Some shapes are symmetrical, some asymmetrical, but all pair shapes consist of two forms that come together to make one balanced shape. A shape may also include weight sharing where one partner supports the other, especially when the shape changes levels.

Mitchell Kearney © 1998

Alonzo King designed these overlapping curves in the torsos for dancers Traci Gilchrest and Hernan Justo.

Warm-Up and Preparation

• Observe selected pictures of sculptures by Henry Moore, Alexander Calder, Joan Miró, or any other 20th-century sculptor that demonstrate interlocking forms. When creating a sculpture, the sculptor looks at the space around the sculpture (the negative, or empty, space) in order to create balance of the mass (positive space, or space with something in it).

• Discuss shapes in nature. Identify interlocking or complementary shapes such as a vine entwining a tree or a rock crystal formation. Identify the positive and negative space you might observe when looking at these forms.

• Review the concept of range of motion covered in chapter 1. The actions of bending (flexion), stretching (extension), and twisting (rotation) lead to the different categories of shapes: angular, curved, twisted, and straight. Explore movement in each of the joints in an isolation exercise as follows:

• Create a series of body-part isolations focusing on just one joint and explore the movement potential and range of motion within this joint. For example, first explore moving only one shoulder. Lift it, drop it, rotate it, and circle it. Try the other. Bend and extend the elbow only. Explore moving the wrist without either the shoulder or elbow. Identify the movements each joint can do. Try the thigh joint, knee, and ankle as well.

• As we learned previously, the two sides of the body work equally to produce symmetry, whereas working the two sides differently produces asymmetry. The teacher will provide a warm-up that includes each of the shapes in a predesigned sequence such as the following:

- Straight shape on high level rising to a balance (symmetrical)
- Low curved shape (symmetrical) resulting in a roll to the floor
- Angled sitting shape using only one side of the body (asymmetrical)
- Spinning turn in place finishing with a symmetrical angled shape with both arms and legs
- Quick rise to another straight shape balancing on one leg on middle level (asymmetrical)
- Transition to a twisted shape on any level then reverse of that shape (asymmetrical)

Traci Gilchrest and Jason Jacobs along with Kati Hanlon Mayo and Tomasz Kumor create the same pair shape, one behind the other. Note the straight lines and angles created by each pair.

EXAMPLE: Chapter 2, Lesson 4A: Shape Gallery

Dwight Rhoden created many pair shapes for the dancers in *Verge*. In this example, selected shapes are caught in stillness and identified using shape words. Watch in each example how the two dancers form one shape together as they move through their different movement phrases. Sometimes more than one pair may demonstrate the same shape; other times only one pair is selected to model a shape.

Structured Improvisations

Improvisation 1: Molding Shapes

• The teacher will choose one class member to be the photographer or will serve in this capacity herself. Using a digital camera, the photographer is

Jason Jacobs supports the weight of Kati Hanlon Mayo during a section of Dwight Rhoden's *Verge*.

responsible for documenting in still pictures as many of the shapes as possible created by the dancers during this exercise.

• Working in pairs, select one partner (A) to close the eyes and stand in a neutral position, representing the sculptor's clay. The other partner (B), the sculptor, takes an arm or leg of partner A and begins to construct a whole-body shape by moving partner A's limbs and torso. The sculptor should try to combine angles and curves and make sure partner A's torso is involved. The finished shape can be on any level or require balancing on one leg.

• Partner B should step away and look at the negative space surrounding the finished shape. Partner A opens the eyes, still holding the shape, while partner B fills the negative space with a shape of her own, combining angles, curves, and twists. Partners should hold the pair shape for a few seconds.

• Partner A then moves away and looks at the shape created by partner B. Partner A creates a new shape to complement and fill in the negative space around partner B.

• Alternate roles in this exercise six to eight times, finding new shapes together.

Improvisation 2: Partner Shapes

In the computer lab, the teacher or class photographer will make prints of the digital pictures taken during the structured improvisations. Each pair should have their own set of six to eight different pictures. The teacher will display all the pictures on the wall to create a shape gallery.

Problem Solving

EXAMPLE: Chapter 2, Lesson 4B: Shapes in Motion

Traci Gilchrest and Benjamin Kubie dance a duet from Dwight Rhoden's *Verge* that demonstrates how two dancers come together to create varied and provocative shapes. The shape types identified in the lesson appear and disappear as the duet progresses.

Pair Shape Studies

• Working with a new partner, select eight shapes from the shape gallery. Because this partnership is new, the shapes will be unfamiliar to one or both of you.

• Sequence the chosen shapes, figure out how to create the shapes together, and make smooth transitions from shape to shape.

- Make sure at least three of the transitions between shapes move through the space with locomotor movement. The Pair Shape study should end in a different location than where it began unless you choose to circle back to the beginning location.
- The teacher should bring in several different pieces of music. Select a piece of music or find a piece of recorded music that suits the study you have created and decide how to count and phrase the Pair Shape study.

From Gallery to Stage

Perform the Pair Shape study for classmates. Dancers in the audience should look to see if they recognize the shapes they created themselves and note the different interpretations and the transitions into the shapes. Performers and audience members should identify the properties of the shapes performed.

Discussion Questions

1. Identify the kinds of shapes that can be formed by two dancers.
2. Define positive and negative space. How does this affect our perception of shapes?

Positive and Negative Space: Sharing a Shape

STATEMENT OF PERFORMANCE

In partners, dancers will create a Pair Shape study inspired by pictures of previous shape improvisations.

Answer each of the following criteria with a yes or no and then score each category from 1 to 5, with 5 being the highest score and 1 the lowest. Use the rubrics to assist in discussion, self-reflection, and assessment of progress in understanding the choreographic concept.

Criteria	Score YES	Score NO
CREATING: PERCEPTUAL SKILLS		
The dancer did the following:		
1. Made eight different pair shapes, including one beginning shape and one ending shape.	_____	_____
2. Transitioned smoothly and logically between shapes.	_____	_____
3. Included three locomotor transitions traveling in space.	_____	_____
4. Each contributed to the choreography.	_____	_____
Creating: Perceptual Skills Total	__________	
PERFORMING: TECHNICAL AND EXPRESSIVE SKILLS		
The dancer did the following:		
1. Accurately reproduced selected movement.	_____	_____
2. Retained strong focus while performing with a partner.	_____	_____
3. Made clear interpretations of selected shapes.	_____	_____
Performing: Technical and Expressive Skills Total	__________	
RESPONDING: INTELLECTUAL AND REFLECTIVE SKILLS		
The dancer did the following:		
1. Discussed choices and identified shapes.	_____	_____
2. Made informed critical observations of own work.	_____	_____
3. Made informed critical observations of the work of others.	_____	_____
4. Noticed and discussed the similarities and different interpretations of shapes selected.	_____	_____
Responding: Intellectual and Reflective Skills Total	__________	

SCORING

5 = Fulfilled all the criteria of creating, performing, and responding in a way that shows a thorough understanding of the skills and concepts to be mastered. Fully participated in the classroom tasks as a performer and as an audience member.

4 = Fulfilled all the criteria but does not yet show a thorough understanding of all skills and concepts. Fully participated in classroom tasks as a performer and as an audience member.

3 = Had difficulty fulfilling the criteria. Was not able to fully complete the assignment. Participated in class but could not complete all tasks as a performer and as an audience member.

2 = Did not complete the assigned work to a satisfactory degree. Did not fully participate as a performer or as an audience member.

1 = Did not participate.

ADDITIONAL COMMENTS

____

____

LESSON 5
BALANCE: SUPPORTING EACH OTHER

© Charles and Mary Love

Amy Earnest and Hernan Justo demonstrate a weight-sharing shape from *Dreamer.* If they were to let go of each other's hands, both would fall. The center of their weight is shared equally between them.

Vocabulary

active weight
counterbalance
gravity
interdependence
lifting
passive weight
supporting
undercurve
weight sharing

Introductory Statement

In the previous lesson, pairs of dancers made shapes together using positive and negative space as a sculptor might. In this lesson, pairs of dancers will move together as one shape, holding hands, to discover balances and weight-sharing shapes requiring one partner to support the other's weight while shifting from one weight-sharing shape to another. The partners support each other and form new shapes in space that could not be maintained without the partner's assistance. Dancers explore moving together and cooperating with each other. They learn to support weight, lift weight, and share weight. The partners learn to understand interdependence in dance. Because these exercises involve weight sharing, dancers must maintain a strong focus to ensure one another's safety.

Warm-Up and Discussion of Weight

- Gravity is the force that draws the body toward the center of the earth. It is related to the concept of weight. In dance, we often ask dancers to give into the weight of a movement, or to feel their weight go down into the earth. This lesson

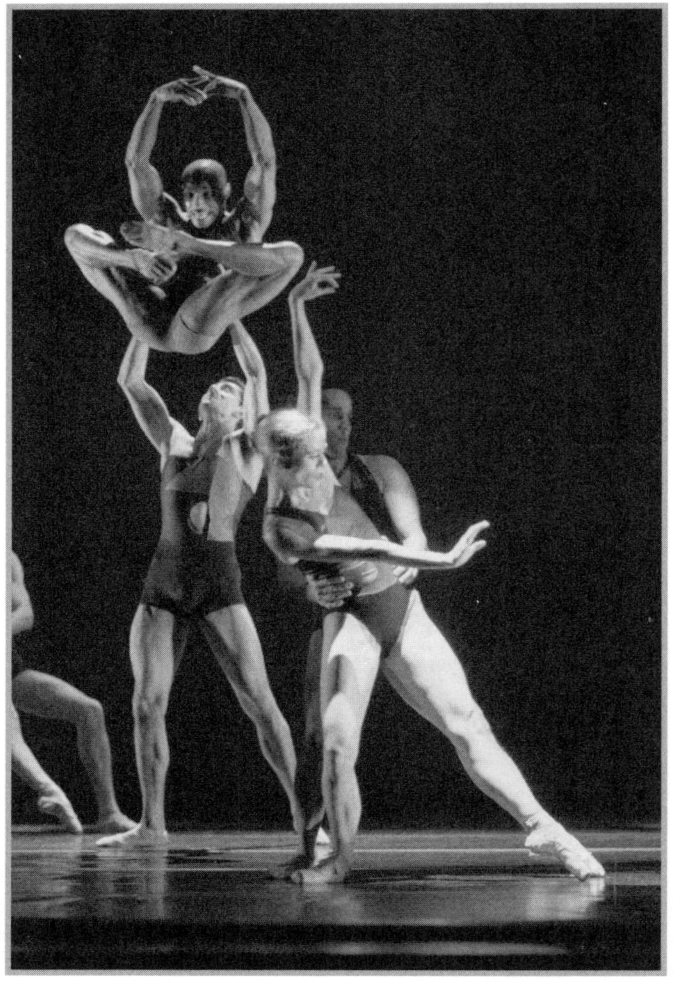

© Rolland Elliott

Uri Sands is lifted into the air by Edgar Vardanian in an exciting moment from *Verge*. Sands assumes a perfectly symmetrical curved shape reminiscent of a ball. It appears as if he will be thrown into the center of the target. He could not maintain this shape in the air for long without the support of his partner.

is about sharing our weight with each other and using shifting and balancing weight to create a movement study. If we give in completely to our body weight, we are using *passive weight.* A passive-weight partner is carried and often must be lifted. When we engage our weight and use it to give a movement more force, we are using *active weight.* Weight in counterbalancing (finding a point of balance between two or more dancers) and in weight sharing (where dancers give weight to one another) is active.

- Begin walking throughout the room, feeling the pull of gravity drawing you down into the floor. Redefine the center of gravity in the body as residing in the pelvis 2 inches below the navel. Consciously lower your body weight into the pelvis to experience heaviness. Give in to the weight passively. You will find it is very hard to move. Your legs may bend so that your walk becomes low and heavy. Now, begin to actively engage the weight by exploring the release and recapturing of the weight in an undercurve from side to side or front to back, shifting the weight from foot to foot. Add arms and explore the feeling of weight in arm swings or figure-eight patterns.

Structured Improvisations

Improvisation 1: Sharing Weight

Find a partner who is similar to you in height and weight. Explore simple weight-sharing exercises. Make sure you really give each other weight, where one partner would fall without the support of the other.

- **Back to back**
    a. Begin by leaning against each other. Slowly begin curving the spine so that the middles of your backs are your support. Wrap arms at the elbows and slowly sink to the floor, sharing weight the whole time. Rise in the same way. Do not disconnect the arms.

b. Standing back to back, partner A gradually bends forward while partner B bends backward until partner B is lying over the back of partner A. Allow partner B's feet to leave the ground before reversing the process to allow the weight of partner A to be completely supported by the back of partner B. At one point the arms may release as well.

- **Wrist to wrist**

  a. Grasp hold of each other's wrists and pull away from each other. Staying straight, slowly extend the arms until you are both leaning away from the center point where the feet are.

  b. Stand an arm's length apart and grasp wrists again. This time curve in the torso so that you pull away from each other at the same time while taking weight into the legs. Both your spines should be equally curved and the legs bent. Pull away until a balance is created and one person would fall if the hands were released. Go lower and higher using the legs to lift the weight.

- **Palms to palms**

  In this exercise, explore how to control weight by facing each other and placing the palms together with the arms extended. Slowly begin to bend your elbows and move closer to each other until your heads touch. Then carefully move outward again, never releasing the pressure of the weight.

- **Shoulder to shoulder**

  Begin by leaning side to side at one shoulder, partner A with the left shoulder touching, partner B with the right shoulder touching. Keep the point of weight shared equally, and smoothly adjust to sharing weight back to back and then on the opposite shoulders. How do you need to adjust your feet to keep sharing the weight between the two of you?

Improvisation 2: Counterbalance

Try a second exploration with the goal of finding pair shapes that include balances and counterbalances while weight sharing. Face and support each other at both wrists. To start, begin to bend the knees and pull away as you balance the weight between you. Eventually release one arm and try different shapes. You may also let one leg come off the ground and try different counterbalanced shapes. Be sure to move slowly, carefully balancing weight between each transition. Create at least four shapes that are weight sharing and balanced with just one arm or on one leg for each dancer.

EXAMPLE: Chapter 2, Lesson 5A: Counterbalanced Duet

Alonzo King works with Hernan Justo, who is portraying the character of Sattva (wisdom and balance), and Servy Gallardo, who is portraying the character of Rajas (energy). In this duet from *Dreamer,* the two forces of energy and balance meet. The duet includes counterbalances and weight sharing. Watch how the shapes and balances of the duet develop as the character of Sattva works hard to contain the energy of Rajas. One dancer would fall without the support of the other.

Improvisation 3: Balance

In this exploration, one dancer is the supporter while the other dancer creates balancing shapes that could not be held without the partner's help. These balancing shapes may be on one leg or supported by the hands. Watch DVD example chapter 2 lesson 5A again and note how the Rajas character balances on one leg in several different shapes. Each pair should make one shape together so that the supporting partner creates a shape that complements the balancing partner's shape. Create at least four of these shapes.

Improvisation 4: Lift and Carry

Explore carrying each other. For example, one dancer may drag the other along the floor. Experiment with several ways to drag each other. Allow one partner to completely support the weight of another by lifting the person. How can one partner carry the other? Begin with the simple weight-sharing exercise of back to back. One dancer flexes her spine forward while the other simply arches backward, keeping all her weight on her partner's back. Sometimes the feet of the dancer resting on top may come off the floor. The supporting partner should try to walk. Each pair should find four different ways to carry or drag each other.

Problem Solving

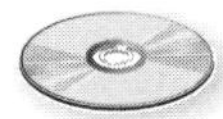

EXAMPLE: Chapter 2, Lesson 5B: Weight Sharing: Finding Active and Passive Weight

In this example from *Dreamer,* we watch Alonzo King present the relationship between Sattva (wisdom and balance), portrayed by Hernan Justo, and Tamas (inertia), portrayed by Amy Earnest. Tamas is heavy and unmotivated to move. Watch the interplay between active and passive weight as Tamas alternately moves and falls. Observe the different ways to carry a partner's weight and the different counterbalanced shapes that evolve.

Weight-Sharing Shapes

Create a Weight-Sharing Shape sequence (see figure 2.6) beginning in a two-person weight-sharing shape. While still connected, move to at least two counterbalanced shapes with one person supporting the balance of the other. Continue to a new supported shape with one partner carrying or dragging the other to a new location. Finally, separate and create a phrase of unsupported mirroring movement, referring to material developed in chapter 2, lesson 3. Find a way to come back together and finish in a counterbalanced ending shape.

Sample Weight-Sharing Shape Sequence

Two-person balanced, connected, symmetrical shape with weight sharing

Still connected, two or more counterbalanced shapes with one person supporting the weight of the other

New supported shape with one partner carrying or dragging the other to a new location

Mirroring sequence unsupported

Two-person balanced, connected, asymmetrical weight-sharing shape

FIGURE 2.6 Start with a two-person weight-sharing shape and end with a counterbalanced ending shape.

Discussion Questions

1. What words can you find to express how it feels when you are in a state of balance aided by someone else?
2. Describe how it feels to support someone and to be supported by someone.
3. Define active and passive weight.
4. How does the use of weight change the look of a movement?

Balance: Supporting Each Other

STATEMENT OF PERFORMANCE

In pairs, dancers will create and perform a Weight-Sharing Shape sequence based on interdependence and using counterbalance, weight sharing, and balance, with a mirroring sequence included.

Answer each of the following criteria with a yes or no and then score each category from 1 to 5, with 5 being the highest score and 1 the lowest. Use the rubrics to assist in discussion, self-reflection, and assessment of progress in understanding the choreographic concept.

Criteria	**Score**	
	YES	NO
CREATING: PERCEPTUAL SKILLS		
The dancer did the following:		
1. Made a sequence of at least five weight-sharing shapes.	_____	_____
2. Moved together through space, carrying and dragging the partner.	_____	_____
3. Developed a mirroring sequence evolving out of the counterbalanced shapes.	_____	_____
4. Contributed equally to the creative process with a partner.	_____	_____
Creating: Perceptual Skills **Total** _____________		
PERFORMING: TECHNICAL AND EXPRESSIVE SKILLS		
The dancer did the following:		
1. Accurately reproduced selected movement.	_____	_____
2. Demonstrated weight sharing throughout the study.	_____	_____
3. Flowed easily from one shape to the next.	_____	_____
4. Retained strong focus to ensure the safety of each partner.	_____	_____
Performing: Technical and Expressive Skills **Total** _____________		
RESPONDING: INTELLECTUAL AND REFLECTIVE SKILLS		
The dancer did the following:		
1. Discussed choices.	_____	_____
2. Made informed critical observations of own work.	_____	_____
3. Made informed critical observations of the work of others.	_____	_____
Responding: Intellectual and Reflective Skills **Total** _____________		

SCORING

5 = Fulfilled all the criteria of creating, performing, and responding in a way that shows a thorough understanding of the skills and concepts to be mastered. Fully participated in the classroom tasks as a performer and as an audience member.

4 = Fulfilled all the criteria but does not yet show a thorough understanding of all skills and concepts. Fully participated in classroom tasks as a performer and as an audience member.

3 = Had difficulty fulfilling the criteria. Was not able to fully complete the assignment. Participated in class but could not complete all tasks as a performer and as an audience member.

2 = Did not complete the assigned work to a satisfactory degree. Did not fully participate as a performer or as an audience member.

1 = Did not participate.

ADDITIONAL COMMENTS

____

____

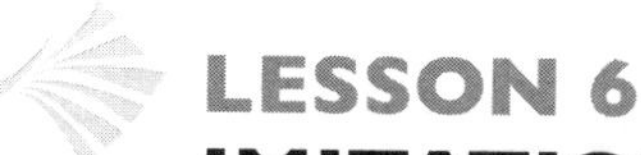

LESSON 6
IMITATION: REFLECTING EACH OTHER

© G. Wagoner

Traci Gilchrest and Kati Hanlon Mayo do the same movement on opposite sides of the stage while Shell Bauman remains in a shape along the vertical reflection line, which divides the stage into right and left sides.

Vocabulary

balance
proscenium
reflection
reflection line
symmetry

Introductory Statement

A choreographer's work is like a three-dimensional painting. The proscenium opening of the stage is the frame of the canvas. A choreographer must place the dancers into the stage in strategically balanced forms that constantly change but are always pleasing to the eyes of the audience. Dividing the stage in half with an imaginary reflection line and placing dancers on opposite sides of that line allows a choreographer to use reflecting forms in space to achieve formal unity. The stage is balanced and at the same time aesthetically pleasing because of the mirroring movement. In this lesson, dancers will experience how movement material can be relocated in the stage space and look different depending on spatial relationships.

EXAMPLE: Chapter 2, Lesson 6A: Balance

This section shows the final shape before the blackout of the section in *Verge* called "Pass Gradually Into." This section includes many different duets that occur together, and Dwight Rhoden has carefully delineated the stage to visually balance the activity. The Impulse character divides the stage vertically into two halves. The two halves are the same. The woman on stage left uses her left leg while the woman on stage right uses her right leg. Symmetry is used here to show closure of this section.

© Rolland Elliott

Dancer Waylon Anderson of North Carolina Dance Theatre2 shows symmetry dividing the stage while teaching this lesson (Imitation: Reflecting Each Other) with middle school students.

Study the pictures of geometric shapes divided in half by a reflection line (see figure 2.7). These shapes are similar to the symmetrical snowflakes created in the children's activity of folding a piece of paper in half and randomly cutting irregular shapes. When the children open the paper, a snowflake appears in which both sides are exactly the same—the shape is symmetrical.

Warm-Up and Preparation

Begin with a mirroring warm-up. Explore air pathways around your body, making diagonal lines as well as carving and piercing lines. Working together as a class, create a movement sequence of 16 counts. Your teacher will choose music in a moderate tempo to complement the exercise. Try dancing the same movements both on the right and left sides of the body. Make sure you include both locomotor and nonlocomotor movements in the phrase.

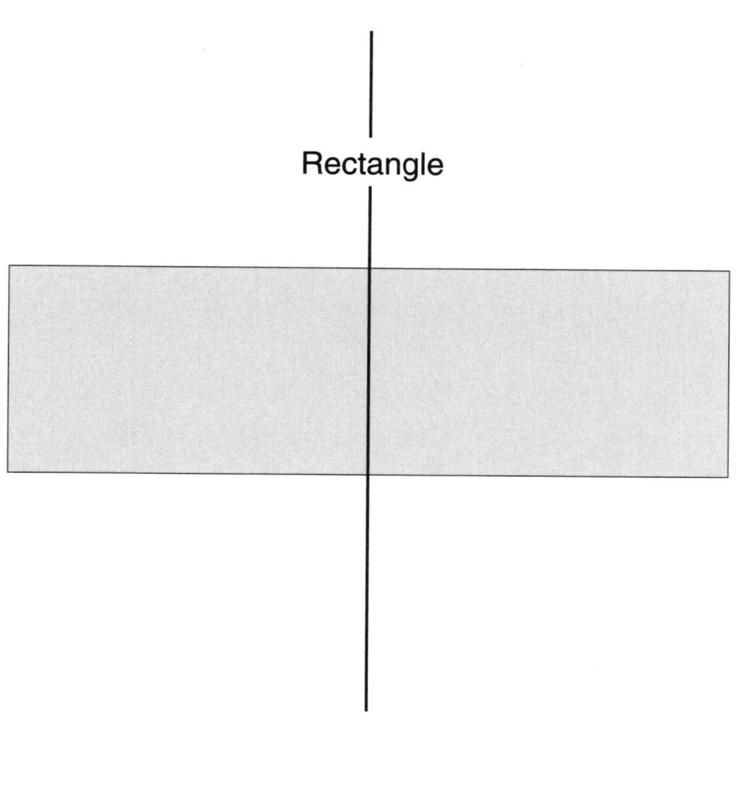

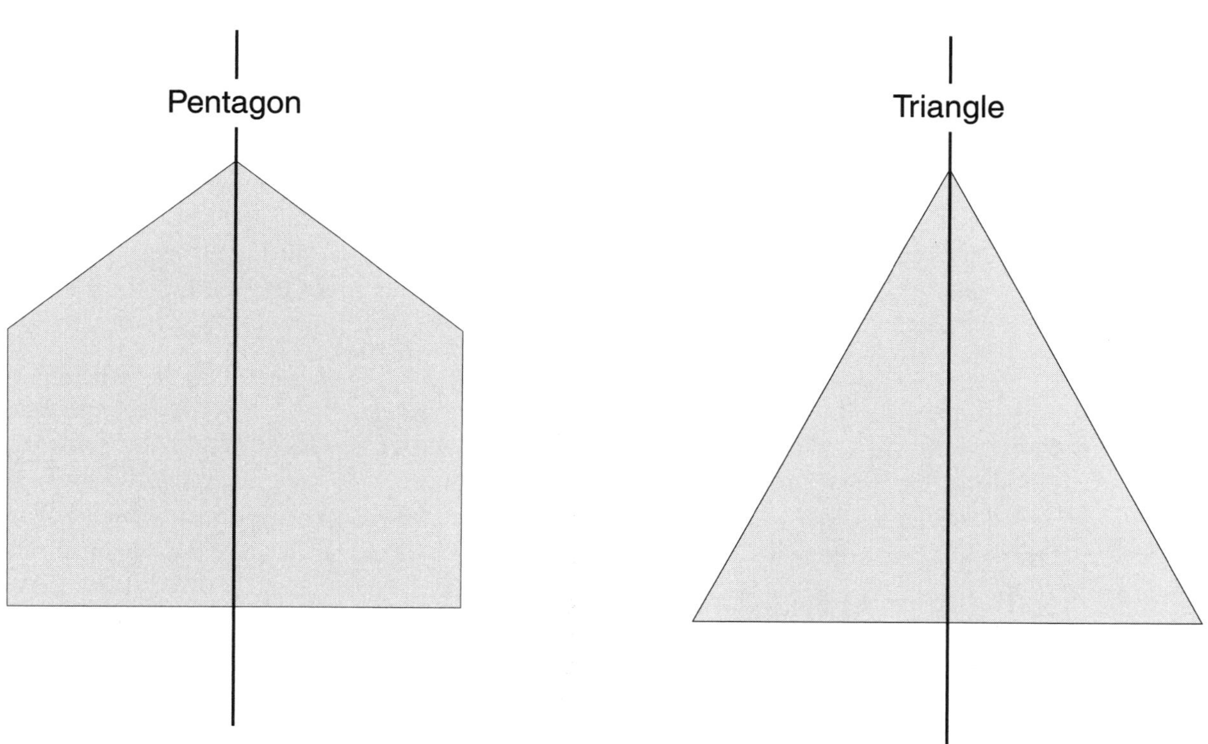

FIGURE 2.7 Geometric shapes divided in half by a reflection line.

Structured Improvisation

Improvisation 1: Reflection

Imagine that the room is divided in half down the center with an invisible reflection line. Work in pairs, with one dancer standing on either side of the line facing forward. Together, perform the 16-count phrase created during the warm-up. The dancer on stage left begins with the left foot and the dancer on stage right begins with the right foot. Repeat the phrase beginning on the opposite foot. Discuss how symmetry is achieved between dancers.

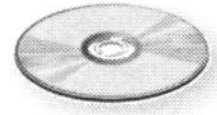

EXAMPLE: Chapter 2, Lesson 6B: "Impulse" Divides the Stage

In this example from *Verge*, the stage is bisected by a reflection line personified by the Impulse character, who moves with slow, symmetrical movements. The other four dancers are moving with the same arms and legs, but on opposite sides of the reflecting line.

Problem Solving

Space Reflection Sequence

- In pairs, create a Space Reflection sequence. After finding a symmetrical starting shape, review the 16-count sequence already learned, and then create an original 16-count phrase that will connect to it. The 32-count sequence will be performed twice.
- The first time through, each dancer stands on opposite sides of the stage, facing front, with an imaginary reflection line dividing the stage vertically into left and right sides. Each dancer starts on a different side (right or left) of the body; that is, the dancer on stage right should start with the left foot, the dancer on stage left with the right foot. Dance the full phrase once in this relationship.

EXAMPLE: Chapter 2, Lesson 6C: Horizontal Reflection Line

In this section from *Verge*, the two main characters, Impulse and Alter Ego, mirror movement using a horizontal reflection line. The Impulse is downstage and the Alter Ego is upstage. It is as if they are describing the center of the target in the middle of the stage space.

- Repeat the phrase, changing stage facings; alternate back to back or do one face to face. You could also change the reflection line to cut the space horizontally, dividing the space into upstage and downstage.
- Find an ending shape that is symmetrical. The completed study will be 64 counts—32 counts with the original phrase, 32 counts with a spatial variation.

Reflections in Space

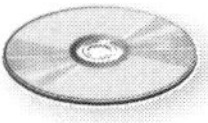

EXAMPLE: Chapter 2, Lesson 6D: Dividing the Space

In this example, the reflection line is clearly vertical and delineated by the Impulse character. Note the mirroring shapes and the balance achieved when the stage is clearly divided into two halves.

Perform the Space Reflection sequences for your classmates. The audience will imagine the position of each reflection line and note the balanced symmetry occurring as they watch the same movement on both sides of the stage at the same time.

Discussion Questions

1. How do we as an audience decide what to look at when many things are happening at one time on stage?
2. Why would a choreographer want to use this type of spatial definition in a dance?
3. What interests you when watching dancers mirror each other?

Imitation: Reflecting Each Other

STATEMENT OF PERFORMANCE

In duets, dancers will create a Space Reflection sequence. Each pair will dance the same movement together but on opposite sides of the stage in a symmetrical reflection.

Answer each of the following criteria with a yes or no and then score each category from 1 to 5, with 5 being the highest score and 1 the lowest. Use the rubrics to assist in discussion, self-reflection, and assessment of progress in understanding the choreographic concept.

Criteria	**Score**	
CREATING: PERCEPTUAL SKILLS	YES	NO
The dancers did the following:		
1. Created a two-person beginning shape, with each dancer on an opposite side of the stage.	_____	_____
2. Created a clear 64-count Space Reflection sequence.	_____	_____
3. Included two different spatial orientations or reflection lines.	_____	_____
4. Created a two-person symmetrical ending shape on opposite sides of the stage.	_____	_____
Creating: Perceptual Skills Total	__________	
PERFORMING: TECHNICAL AND EXPRESSIVE SKILLS		
The dancers did the following:		
1. Accurately reproduced selected movement.	_____	_____
2. Moved with an awareness of the partner so that all shapes and relationships were clear.	_____	_____
3. Smoothly transitioned between the phrases.	_____	_____
Performing: Technical and Expressive Skills Total	__________	
RESPONDING: INTELLECTUAL AND REFLECTIVE SKILLS		
The dancers did the following:		
1. Discussed choices.	_____	_____
2. Made informed critical observations of own work.	_____	_____
3. Made informed critical observations of the work of others.	_____	_____
4. Noticed and discussed the similarities and differences between spatial usage.	_____	_____
Responding: Intellectual and Reflective Skills Total	__________	

SCORING

5 = Fulfilled all the criteria of creating, performing, and responding in a way that shows a thorough understanding of the skills and concepts to be mastered. Fully participated in the classroom tasks as a performer and as an audience member.

4 = Fulfilled all the criteria but does not yet show a thorough understanding of all skills and concepts. Fully participated in classroom tasks as a performer and as an audience member.

3 = Had difficulty fulfilling the criteria. Was not able to fully complete the assignment. Participated in class but could not complete all tasks as a performer and as an audience member.

2 = Did not complete the assigned work to a satisfactory degree. Did not fully participate as a performer or as an audience member.

1 = Did not participate.

ADDITIONAL COMMENTS

____

____

LESSON 7
PROBLEM SOLVING: CREATING A DUET

Vocabulary

duet

Mitchell Kearner © 1997

Alonzo King rehearses with Mia Cunningham and Shell Bauman as they demonstrate a counterbalanced shape.

Introductory Statement

In the previous six lessons, structured improvisations led to short movement studies that introduced important concepts relating to space. These spatial concepts include air and floor pathways, diagonals, mirroring and weight sharing (interpersonal space), positive and negative space, and reflections (symmetry and asymmetry) balancing space. Using the material explored in the previous lessons, dancers will create original duets.

Creating a Duet

A duet is about the shared space of two dancers. Their relationship with each other and the shapes they form in space heighten our visual interest as they move. You have already created six different studies—an Air to Floor Pathway dance, Diagonal dance, Reflection duet, Pair Shape study, Weight Sharing Shape sequence,

© Rolland Elliott

© Rolland Elliott

In these three pictures from Dwight Rhoden's *Verge,* we can see a variety of pair shapes. In the first picture, Edgar Vardanian and Uri Sands share each other's weight as they push and pull themselves through the space. In the second picture, Jason Jacobs supports Kati Hanlon Mayo in a lifted, counterbalanced shape. In the third picture, Benjamin Kubie carries Traci Gilchrest from one spot to another.

© Rolland Elliott

and Space Reflection sequence—each based on a different spatial concept and spatial relationship. Working in pairs, choose one of the studies as a starting point for creating a duet 5 to 6 minutes in length. Depending on the chosen theme, you may use whichever material you developed previously as a starting point.

Following are some examples of themes for the duet:

1. **Ego and Alter Ego or Me and My Shadow.** In *Verge,* Dwight Rhoden introduced two lead characters, the Impulse and his Alter Ego. The two characters are presented in several different mirroring sequences. They also reflect each other in space, dancing the same movements but on opposite sides of the stage. In this way, the two characters maintain their relationship even when they are not together.

EXAMPLE: Chapter 2, Lesson 7A: Last Moments of *Verge*

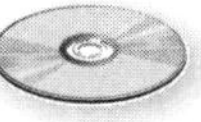

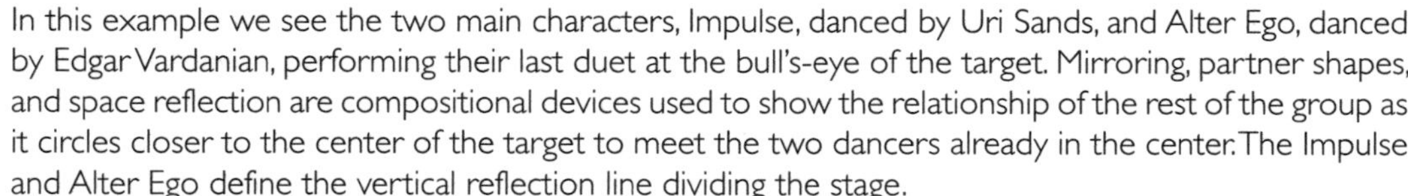

In this example we see the two main characters, Impulse, danced by Uri Sands, and Alter Ego, danced by Edgar Vardanian, performing their last duet at the bull's-eye of the target. Mirroring, partner shapes, and space reflection are compositional devices used to show the relationship of the rest of the group as it circles closer to the center of the target to meet the two dancers already in the center. The Impulse and Alter Ego define the vertical reflection line dividing the stage.

2. **Game of Statues or Tag.** Alonzo King was inspired by children's games when he created an interdependent duet in *Chants.* In this duet, the two dancers must remain attached throughout the whole duet. They support each other and help one another to balance in unusual positions.

EXAMPLE: Chapter 2, Lesson 7B: Playful Duet

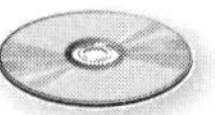

This duet, choreographed to a children's song from Africa, presents Traci Gilchrest and Anita Sun Pacylowski in a duet that requires them to stay connected at the hands throughout. They counterbalance in symmetrical shapes and work in both literal and lateral mirroring. They dance side by side and facing each other. Sometimes they move in space, and sometimes they circle one another. At the end, they form a counterbalanced shape resulting in a quick exit from the stage.

3. **Contrasting Characters.** In three duets from *Dreamer,* King explores weight sharing, supporting, lifting, and counterbalance. He depicts the interplay of three different energies *(gunas)* personified by the forces of Sattva (balance and wisdom), Tamas (inertia), and Rajas (dynamism and energy) found in Hindu thought. These forces act on the creative idea until it is born to reality.

EXAMPLE: Chapter 2, Lesson 7C: Three Gunas

The first duet presented is between Rajas (dynamism and energy), danced by Servy Gallardo, and Sattva (balance and wisdom), danced by Hernan Justo. Sattva tries to contain the energy of Rajas by holding him in place. They weight share and counterbalance in a variety of movements and shapes until Rajas is subdued and leaves the stage.

Next, Sattva moves to Tamas (inertia and ignorance), danced by Amy Earnest. She must be awakened and coaxed into movement. She personifies passivity and heaviness. Sattva must carry and lift her into motion until she can move away by herself.

Last, Sattva dances with the Dreamer, or "creative idea," coaxing her to awaken and begin her emergence into the world. He has brought the forces of inertia and energy into balance.

Problem Solving: Creating a Duet

STATEMENT OF PERFORMANCE

In pairs, dancers will create and perform a duet based on the movement material explored in the first six lessons in chapter 2.

Answer each of the following criteria with a yes or no and then score each category from 1 to 5, with 5 being the highest score and 1 the lowest. Use the rubrics to assist in discussion, self-reflection, and assessment of progress in understanding the choreographic concept.

Criteria	**Score** YES	NO
CREATING: PERCEPTUAL SKILLS		
The dancers did the following:		
1. Selected and developed movement material explored in the previous six lessons.	_____	_____
2. Selected an appropriate guiding idea.	_____	_____
3. Found creative solutions to order movement material selected.	_____	_____
4. Clearly structured a beginning, middle, and end.	_____	_____
5. Showed spatial variety and changing relationships in a duet.	_____	_____
6. Collaborated with a partner to make movement choices.	_____	_____
Creating: Perceptual Skills Total	__________	
PERFORMING: TECHNICAL AND EXPRESSIVE SKILLS		
The dancers did the following:		
1. Accurately performed selected movement.	_____	_____
2. Made smooth transitions from one movement to another.	_____	_____
3. Danced as a duet with awareness of one another.	_____	_____
Performing: Technical and Expressive Skills Total	__________	
RESPONDING: INTELLECTUAL AND REFLECTIVE SKILLS		
The dancers did the following:		
1. Discussed choices.	_____	_____
2. Made informed critical observations of own work.	_____	_____
3. Made informed critical observations of the work of others.	_____	_____
Responding: Intellectual and Reflective Skills Total	__________	

SCORING

5 = Fulfilled all the criteria of creating, performing, and responding in a way that shows a thorough understanding of the skills and concepts to be mastered. Fully participated in the classroom tasks as a performer and as an audience member.

4 = Fulfilled all the criteria but does not yet show a thorough understanding of all skills and concepts. Fully participated in classroom tasks as a performer and as an audience member.

3 = Had difficulty fulfilling the criteria. Was not able to fully complete the assignment. Participated in class but could not complete all tasks as a performer and as an audience member.

2 = Did not complete the assigned work to a satisfactory degree. Did not fully participate as a performer or as an audience member.

1 = Did not participate.

ADDITIONAL COMMENTS

____

____

Student Self-Evaluation Questions

Name: ________________________ Date: ______________ Class: ______________

CREATIVE ASSIGNMENT

1. What is the most interesting spatial decision that you and your partner made?

2. What was the most challenging problem you had to solve while you were working together?

3. How did you solve the creative problem together? Describe the process.

4. What did you learn about yourself as a collaborator while you were trying to solve the problem?

5. What was the role of improvisation in generating material for your study?

6. How did you decide on the structure for your dance?

7. What is another project or experience that might grow out of this one?

Chapter 3

Time: Exploring Tempo

© Ilya Margolis

Amy Earnest, personifying inertia in *Dreamer,* is pulled into action by the other dancers. Her movement is slow and heavy as if she were awakening from a deep sleep.

OVERVIEW

In this chapter, explorations in the compositional component of time as defined on a continuum of fast or slow will introduce how a choreographer might use tempo, the pace of movement. Acceleration, or gradually building in speed, is an effective way of using tempo to increase movement intensity. When the concepts of acceleration and deceleration were first introduced in chapter 1, lesson 3, a phrase of gestures was gradually accelerated and decelerated. These concepts will be further developed as dancers explore how to gradually accelerate a whole movement study, not just one phrase.

The five lessons in this chapter encourage movement exploration in slow motion, quick motion, slow and fast motion together, and acceleration. The culminating choreographic study challenges trios of dancers to use the element of time and its acceleration to add color and interest to movement phrases.

Alonzo King arrived in Charlotte, North Carolina, in 1999 to create his ballet *Chants* for North Carolina Dance Theatre. He began his rehearsal by stating that if music is thought made audible, then dance is thought made visible. In other words, dance provides a separate but equal layer or contrapuntal voice to a piece of music. King's new ballet would use African chants that were free in structure and uneven in phrasing. The dance lines were choreographed to move over and around the music, complementing it and adding unique visual parameters to the music.

Another part of the information is forcing yourself to be uncomfortable. You learn good stuff.

ALONZO KING, 1999

Rolland Elliott

Rebecca Carmazzi is lifted to a moment of stillness during a performance of *Verge* by Dwight Rhoden.

Dance sequences were created and rehearsed without music, and only after the movement phrases were learned was the music coordinated with the dance. Sometimes counts were used, but often not even counts were present. The dancers were shown or told what movement to do, and they experimented with the timing and look of the phrase until King saw what he wanted and then finalized it. The concept of time became interplay between slow and fast movements and their relationship to an established pulse.

LESSON 1
SLOW MOTION: DANCING IN REVERIE

Introductory Statement

Motion produced without a time frame often does not offer an accurate sense of the length of this time. Usually, we do not notice how fast or slow we make a movement; we simply do what we need to do. The motivation for the movement determines a subjective measurement of time. In dance, however, the choreographer consciously strives to control the timing of movement. Often pulses played in music determine how fast or slow a movement ought to be danced. The manipulation of time is an important part of dance composition.

Choreographer Alonzo King prefers to allow dancers to find the innate tempo of a movement phrase before introducing counts or pulses. He believes that the body makes its own music. Only after constructing a movement phrase and teaching it to his dancers does he add the auditory line, the music.

Vocabulary

adagio
dab
environment
float
glide
lightness
pulse
soft
suspend
sustained movement
tempo
weightlessness

Warm-Up and Identifying Pulse and Slowness

- After finding your pulse in your wrist or neck, begin walking around the room in rhythm with your pulse. Notice that not all footfalls will be together because not all pulses are the same. Continue to walk. Gradually begin to follow the beat of a drum (provided by the teacher) so that all footfalls are now performed in a moderate tempo. Change the pulse so that it is quicker than the moderate walk and continue until all footfalls move quite fast. Revert once again to the moderate tempo. Change the tempo one more time to an adagio requiring slow, determined movement. Move back to the moderate walking tempo. Discuss how the body feels in a slow tempo as opposed to a fast tempo. Determine personal preferences.
- In a slow tempo, guided by a triangle or bell, find nonlocomotor movement that is sustained (slow and smooth). Discuss action words such as *float, glide,* and *suspend.* Discuss descriptive words such as *soft, light,* or *weak* (depending on the use of weight). Move through space using simple locomotor movement to float, glide, and suspend throughout the space. The teacher will provide a piece of music in a slow tempo to continue the improvisation. Explore changing levels while moving slowly as well as while moving quickly through the space. Sometimes we may move in a sustained fashion using more weight. Explore slowness with heaviness and explore pressing, wringing, and sinking in movement. Discuss the

differences between moving slowly while varying the use of weight from light to heavy.

- Discuss the concepts of timelessness, weightlessness, and spatial void evoked by a dream. What might it be like to be inside a dream, that place of unusual space and time? The dream is a new place. How do you respond? Are you careful, cautious, or wary? Or do you float gently through the emptiness?
- Discuss learning and experiencing things for the first time. How might this be shown in movement?

Structured Improvisation

Improvisation 1: Exploring a Dream

Take a minute to visualize a recent pleasant dream. Think of the location, the characters, and your role. Improvising and using sustained movement only, re-create in movement selected moments from the dream. For example, Alonzo King created a dream about joy and newness in *Dreamer.* Prepare your own script as needed.

Dream Sequence From *Dreamer*

Perform an awakening stretch.

Discover the arms in space, creating air pathways around the body.

Discover locomotion with simple movement into space.

Explore the floor with simple crawls and touches.

Rise into the space and gently push away a cloud or drape.

Gently move throughout all four corners of the stage.

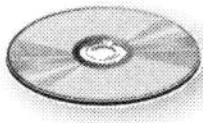

EXAMPLE: Chapter 3, Lesson 1A: The Dreamer

In this solo from *Dreamer,* the main character, Dreamer, awakens into a new world. The dancer, Mia Cunningham, must retain a dreamlike quality in her sustained, light movements. Note how smooth and soft the movement appears, even when there are short spurts of faster dabbing movement. The solo is light and dreamlike.

Improvisation 2: Creating an Imaginary Voyage

- Imagine the dance space is on the moon. Get off the spaceship and begin to move in this environment. Show weightlessness by floating and gliding through space. Vary the size of gestures from large to small. Use a variety of locomotor and nonlocomotor movements such as turning, lunging, walking, and balancing as you traverse the space from one side of the room to the other. All the territory is new and requires exploration.
- During this exploration of the moon, collect four objects of varying sizes from different parts of the room and carry them as souvenirs. Find a unique way each time to gather what you choose to take with you. Place the objects in a pocket, a knapsack, or under your arm. Remember that the objects have no weight either.
- Begin the journey all together as a class and simply explore moving in this environment. Don't worry about how much time it takes to cross the room.

Improvisation 3: Sharing the Trek

• Half the group performs the improvised imaginary voyage for the other half. Dancers should move in their own time, collecting their found objects independently. The teacher should choose suitable music to set an atmosphere. Respond to musical sound as you hear it for the first time, but continue to move independently of it.

• Discuss how it feels to remain in a slow and sustained movement language for an extended period of time. Also discuss what an audience member will experience while watching slow, sustained movement. How did the addition of music affect the movement?

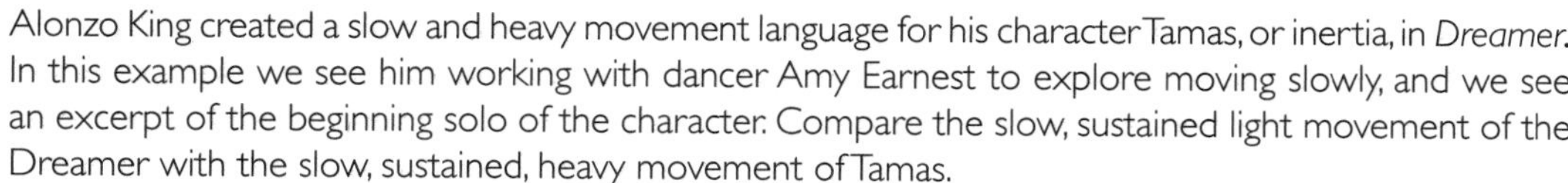

Problem Solving

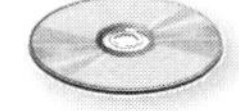

EXAMPLE: Chapter 3, Lesson 1B: Moving Slowly

Alonzo King created a slow and heavy movement language for his character Tamas, or inertia, in *Dreamer*. In this example we see him working with dancer Amy Earnest to explore moving slowly, and we see an excerpt of the beginning solo of the character. Compare the slow, sustained light movement of the Dreamer with the slow, sustained, heavy movement of Tamas.

Constructing a Dance Environment

• In groups of four, or quartets, randomly draw an environment card from a hat (see figure 3.1). Each quartet must turn the whole room into that environment, identifying it with movement only. Because this is the first time entering the environment, limit the initial movement vocabulary to slow, sustained movement unless attacked or threatened by something that might warrant a quick change or escape.

• Depending on the environment, the use of weight may change to include slower and heavier or stronger sustained movement as well as light floating and gliding movement.

• All four members of the quartet should move through the space at the same time. Start anywhere in the room and explore all parts of the environment. Do not use literal pantomime, but rather select movement to expand into dance. Design a walk or specific locomotor movement for traveling through each environment, and design a way to change levels to join together at some point. Each dancer should collect four souvenirs and develop the collecting gestures into dance movement.

Sample Environments

Dark jungle—vines, rain, uneven terrain, quicksand
Deep cave—hidden waterfall, slippery rocks, uneven ledges, stones in the way
Underwater—coral reef, anemones, fish sweeping by, sponges, sand
Desert—hot sand, sand dunes, hot winds, single tree
Glacier—slippery ice, frozen wind, gentle snowfall, snowdrifts, silent footsteps

FIGURE 3.1 You may use these sample environments to draw from a hat.

- Dancers should begin offstage and exit the stage at the end. The stage becomes alive only when the first dancer appears. The adventure should last from 1 to 3 minutes. The dancers are responsible for crafting their own phrase traversing the environment.

Sharing the Experience

In quartets, perform the Dance Environments for each other. Dancers should bring in different kinds of music selections that they feel might suit their environments. From the variety of selections brought in, each group should choose music that will form a sound environment for the performance.

Discussion Questions

1. Try to imagine what it would be like to move within a dream. What would the dream world be like?
2. Can you do things in a dream that you cannot do when you are awake?
3. Share how you feel when waking from a dream.
4. What is a nightmare? Are the movement qualities and emotions different in dreams and nightmares?

Slow Motion: Dancing in Reverie

STATEMENT OF PERFORMANCE

In quartets, dancers will create an imaginary environment while demonstrating slow, sustained movements and finding ways to depict reactions to the environment.

Answer each of the following criteria with a yes or no and then score each category from 1 to 5, with 5 being the highest score and 1 the lowest. Use the rubrics to assist in discussion, self-reflection, and assessment of progress in understanding the choreographic concept.

Criteria	Score	
CREATING: PERCEPTUAL SKILLS The dancers did the following:	YES	NO
1. Made clear slow, sustained locomotor and nonlocomotor movement selections.	_____	_____
2. Entered and exited the environment in character.	_____	_____
3. Made good spatial decisions for the group.	_____	_____
4. Collected four specific artifacts.	_____	_____
Creating: Perceptual Skills Total	__________	
PERFORMING: TECHNICAL AND EXPRESSIVE SKILLS The dancers did the following:		
1. Accurately reproduced selected movement.	_____	_____
2. Demonstrated slow, sustained movement.	_____	_____
3. Retained strong focus throughout the environment.	_____	_____
4. Maintained a clear group relationship in the space.	_____	_____
Performing: Technical and Expressive Skills Total	__________	
RESPONDING: INTELLECTUAL AND REFLECTIVE SKILLS The dancers did the following:		
1. Discussed choices.	_____	_____
2. Made informed critical observations of own work.	_____	_____
3. Made informed critical observations of the work of others.	_____	_____
Responding: Intellectual and Reflective Skills Total	__________	

SCORING

5 = Fulfilled all the criteria of creating, performing, and responding in a way that shows a thorough understanding of the skills and concepts to be mastered. Fully participated in the classroom tasks as a performer and as an audience member.

4 = Fulfilled all the criteria but does not yet show a thorough understanding of all skills and concepts. Fully participated in classroom tasks as a performer and as an audience member.

3 = Had difficulty fulfilling the criteria. Was not able to fully complete the assignment. Participated in class but could not complete all tasks as a performer and as an audience member.

2 = Did not complete the assigned work to a satisfactory degree. Did not fully participate as a performer or as an audience member.

1 = Did not participate.

ADDITIONAL COMMENTS

____

____

LESSON 2
SPEED: LEARNING TO DANCE QUICKLY

Vocabulary

allegro
compound time
duple meter
locomotor movement

Introductory Statement

Quick movement sequences provide unique technical challenges. A dancer must be able to shift weight from foot to foot and to a new direction effortlessly and cleanly. The dancer must coordinate all body parts efficiently so that the shape and line of the movement is not lost in spite of the swiftness of the tempo. Creating original movement phrases in a fast tempo can also provide unique challenges for the choreographer. Many dancers moving quickly throughout the stage require clear pathways in space, definite movement counts to keep them dancing together, interweaving movement sequences that give them enough space in which to dance, and carefully planned locomotor movement sequences that incorporate directional changes.

Locomotor movements are sometimes categorized as even and uneven. Locomotor movements that are even take an equal amount of time to perform each part. For instance, each foot in a run or walk is placed on the ground for the same amount of time, and we usually count the movement as 1, 2 or 1, 2, 3, 4 (duple meter). Uneven locomotor movements take an uneven amount of time to perform separate parts. In a skip, a quick hop is followed by a slower step. In a gallop, the first forward step takes a longer amount of time than the shorter closing step. Such movements combining long with short are uneven. They are accompanied by 6/8 or compound time that allows 2 beats for the longer part and 1 beat for the shorter.

© Rolland Elliott

Kati Hanlon Mayo and Jason Jacobs perform a quick duet in Dwight Rhoden's *Verge*. They are caught in the middle of their forward movement across the stage. Even though the movement is swift, the dancers retain clean lines and body shapes.

Warm-Up and Tempo

• Begin walking throughout the dance space to the steady beat of a drum or to selected music. A drumming dancer should provide a pulse that gradually accelerates until the dancers are jogging and then running. Change directions and move backward and sideways during the improvisation. Dodge each other to avoid collisions. Stay alert, watching out for others.

• The drummer should divide the beat into groups of 8 counts. Began to prance (either in space or in one spot) for 8 counts and then jump for 8 counts. Repeat several times until everyone is comfortable.

• The drummer will change the meter to a brisk 6/8 time. Create a simple skipping, sliding, and galloping phrase such as four skips forward, four slides sideways, and four gallops in a circle. Vary the direction of the skips or gallops.

• Discuss duple and compound time and locomotor movements that are traditionally performed in either time frame.

Duple (2s and 4s)	**Compound (6/8)**
Walk	Skip
Run or jog	Slide (sideways)
Prance	Gallop
Jump	
Hop	
Stag leap	

• Create a word sequence of locomotor movements to be performed in duple time that can be repeated, such as step hop, step leap, step jump, jump with a turn, and hop with a turn. Interpret the locomotor words individually. The phrase should only move forward in space. Design arm movements to complement the chosen locomotor movements. A quick tempo should be set by the drummer.

Structured Improvisation

EXAMPLE: Chapter 3, Lesson 2A: Moving Quickly

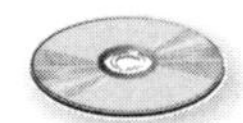

In this excerpt of a performance of Alonzo King's *Dreamer,* the stage is alive with activity spurred on by the Rajas character. Each group moves at lightning speed and exits and enters when the phrase finishes. Watch the different locomotor movements. The music and movement is in duple time.

Improvisation 1: Sequencing Space and Time

Beginning at one corner of the room, perform the original phrase created in the warm-up across the floor, repeating it until you are offstage. For example:

1 2 3 4 5 6 7 8

Step hop, step leap, step jump, jump turn, hop with a turn

Dancers follow each other, one person entering after every 8 counts. Each dancer's phrase will be slightly different because original movements of the arms and legs have been created to correspond to the action words.

Improvisation 2: My Own Time

• For the second entrance, create an original 8-count locomotor movement phrase that moves forward in space across the stage. Only two of the movements from the previous phrase may be used. Practice the phrase and make sure it can be repeated. Practice dancing both phrases one after the other. The phrase is now 16 counts, using the 8-count phrase (A) from improvisation 1, Sequencing Space and Time, and this 8-count phrase (B).

• Drumming or clapping provides a brisk tempo. Beginning at a corner of the room, move across the space dancing phrase A as many times as necessary until reaching the other side. After all have crossed, recross the space performing phrase B.

Problem Solving

EXAMPLE: Chapter 3, Lesson 2B: "Women of Butela"

Watch how the women in this section of Alonzo King's *Chants* move quickly through the space, as if they were birds in flight. Note the exits and entrances and the speed of the locomotion that is structured in duple time. Identify the different kinds of locomotor movement.

Soaring and Swooping

The challenge of this lesson is for all dancers to do both movement phrases across the stage space roughly at the same time. In order to do this, each dancer must select a specific pathway. Start anywhere offstage, but design the pathway for a stage crossing. Reenter from somewhere else and make another crossing. There will always be at least two people starting from different spots offstage and dancing on the stage at the same time. There may be as many as eight dancers or even more on stage at the same time. The image for the dance sequence might be a flock of birds randomly flying over an open field to escape an impending storm.

Where Am I Going?

As a class, post a large piece of paper on the wall. Draw an individual pathway for each dancer's crossings on the paper (the score). If possible, select a different color to represent the pathway of each dancer. After finishing the score, rehearse the dance. Make sure everyone exits completely after each crossing of the stage. When the rehearsal is finished, look for intersecting pathways and decide the order of performance for each dancer. Assign each pathway a number that signifies the order. Stagger entrances and exits.

Flocking Onstage

• After pathways are set and order of performance decided, rehearse the sequences slowly to make sure there will be no accidents.

• The teacher will provide a piece of music that is allegro or instruct the accompanist to play an allegro improvisation to allow the dancers an opportunity to individually rehearse their phrases to the music.

• When the dancers are ready, perform the whole sequence of individual phrases throughout the space.

Bird Watching

• Discuss the challenges of moving quickly with a larger group of people.

• Divide into two groups so that half may watch and the other half dance. Decide who will be in what group by consulting the pathway drawings on the board and your experience dancing with each other in the previous exercise. Try to make the most visually interesting combination of phrases.

Discussion Questions

1. What motivates us into action, or to move from place to place?
2. In the different movement phrases created for this assignment, identify your preferred locomotor movement.
3. What are the challenges of moving quickly?
4. When you watch a group of dancers moving quickly, what emotions do they reveal?

Speed: Learning to Dance Quickly

STATEMENT OF PERFORMANCE

Dancers will each create two 8-count phrases of locomotor movement in a fast tempo that can be performed across the stage space along with other dancers.

Answer each of the following criteria with a yes or no and then score each category from 1 to 5, with 5 being the highest score and 1 the lowest. Use the rubrics to assist in discussion, self-reflection, and assessment of progress in understanding the choreographic concept.

Criteria	**Score**	
CREATING: PERCEPTUAL SKILLS	YES	NO
The dancers did the following:		
1. Made logical spatial decisions to avoid others.	_____	_____
2. Created two separate 8-count phrases.	_____	_____
3. Repeated movement phrases accurately.	_____	_____
Creating: Perceptual Skills Total	__________	
PERFORMING: TECHNICAL AND EXPRESSIVE SKILLS		
The dancers did the following:		
1. Accurately reproduced selected movement.	_____	_____
2. Moved clearly at a fast pace.	_____	_____
3. Flowed easily from one movement phrase to the other.	_____	_____
4. Retained strong focus throughout the performance to avoid collisions.	_____	_____
Performing: Technical and Expressive Skills Total	__________	
RESPONDING: INTELLECTUAL AND REFLECTIVE SKILLS		
The dancers did the following:		
1. Discussed choices.	_____	_____
2. Made informed critical observations of own work.	_____	_____
3. Made informed critical observations of the work of others.	_____	_____
4. Noticed and discussed the similarities and differences in the different phrases.	_____	_____
Responding: Intellectual and Reflective Skills Total	__________	

SCORING

5 = Fulfilled all the criteria of creating, performing, and responding in a way that shows a thorough understanding of the skills and concepts to be mastered. Fully participated in the classroom tasks as a performer and as an audience member.

4 = Fulfilled all the criteria but does not yet show a thorough understanding of all skills and concepts. Fully participated in classroom tasks as a performer and as an audience member.

3 = Had difficulty fulfilling the criteria. Was not able to fully complete the assignment. Participated in class but could not complete all tasks as a performer and as an audience member.

2 = Did not complete the assigned work to a satisfactory degree. Did not fully participate as a performer or as an audience member.

1 = Did not participate.

ADDITIONAL COMMENTS

____

____

____

LESSON 3
PACING: COMBINING DIFFERENT PULSES

Introductory Statement

Within a piece of music there may be two pulse rates, one moderate and one twice as slow (half time). Occasionally, there may even be a third ongoing beat that moves faster than the first two beats (double time). A choreographer may choose one of the three rates to make the basic pulse for the choreography.

______ ______ ______ ______ **half time**

___ ___ ___ ___ ___ ___ ___ ___ **basic (moderate) pulse**

_ _ _ _ _ _ _ _ _ _ _ _ _ _ _ _ **double time**

In a dance work, tempo changes are frequent. They may denote a change of section within the work or provide clues as to the characters in the work. For instance, dancers often show two different interpretations of the tempo at the same time. In tap dance, a dancer may set a simple tempo and then dance it in half time (twice as slow as the pulse) or double time (twice as fast) in order to achieve rhythmic interest.

Vocabulary

adagio
allegro
beat
dancer counts
double time
half time
pulse
tempo

Benjamin Kubie and Alex Donovan remain motionless while Edgar Vardanian moves slowly through symmetrical shapes and Uri Sands moves as quickly as possible in large asymmetrical shapes during the final section of Dwight Rhoden's *Verge*.

Warm-Up: Moving With the Pulse

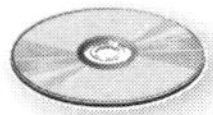

EXAMPLE: Chapter 3, Lesson 3A: Demonstrating Fast and Slow

Alonzo King demonstrates his interpretation of the time continuum of fast and slow by asking Heather Maloy to dance a phrase from *Dreamer* as quickly as possible and then as slowly as possible. Watch how the movement changes.

- The teacher sets a steady pulse with a drum. Begin walking exactly on the drum beats. Move throughout the space but never lose the pulse. Explore moving forward, backward, sideways, and with turns.
- Now move only in half time, or twice as slow as the pulse. The drum will maintain the previous pulse while the dancers move twice as slowly. Moving through space, walk in the same way but note the effort of maintaining movement that uses half time as its pulse. Explore lunging, stretching, and leg extensions.
- While the same pulse on the drum continues, move in double time, or twice as fast. Note the challenges of maintaining the quick tempo. Explore jumping, running, and hopping.
- Divide into two groups. One group dances in half time and the other in double time while the drum maintains the pulse. After some time, change roles.

Structured Improvisation

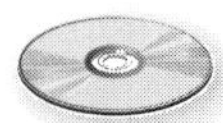

EXAMPLE: Chapter 3, Lesson 3B: Slow With Fast

In "Women of Butela" from *Chants,* Alonzo King puts slow and fast movement together. The chorus moves slowly, essentially in one spot, at the back of the stage, while the soloist, Anita Sun Pacylowski, moves quickly with locomotor movement patterns at the front of the stage.

Improvisation 1: An Adagio

Create an original dance phrase in an adagio tempo. In the warm-up, you improvised moving slowly with simple locomotor movement in half time to the drum pulse. For this adagio phrase, use only nonlocomotor movement such as stretching and balancing with leg extensions. Coordinate arms and legs as they move slowly, describing space and finding air pathways. Each dancer should develop a dance phrase of 16 dancer counts, which will amount to 32 pulse counts. The phrase should not move much in space and should be repeated on the other side, perhaps changing directions. The teacher will play a selected pulse on the drum while the dancers perform their adagio phrases in half time against the pulse.

Dancer Counts

_____	_____	_____	_____	_____	_____	_____	_____
1 (2)	2 (2)	3 (2)	4 (2)	5 (2)	6 (2)	7 (2)	8 (2)
_____	_____	_____	_____	_____	_____	_____	_____
9 (2)	10 (2)	11 (2)	12 (2)	13 (2)	14 (2)	15 (2)	16 (2)

Drum Beats

1	2	3	4	5	6	7	8	9	10	11	12	13	14	15	16
17	18	19	20	21	22	23	24	25	26	27	28	29	30	31	32

Improvisation 2: Adagio in Half Time

- Divide into two groups. The audience half of the class will provide the pulse by clapping softly and the dancer half will perform its adagio phrases in half time to the pulse beat.
- Switch roles. Discuss the challenges of maintaining a slower pulse than the accompaniment.

Improvisation 3: An Allegro

Discuss double time once more. Using some of the movement phrases developed in lesson 2 of this chapter, create a movement phrase of locomotor movements or foot rhythms that will consist of 32 dancer counts to 16 pulse counts that will be danced double time. Make sure the phrase can be repeated. The teacher will play a selected pulse on the drum while the dancers perform their locomotor phrases double time.

Dancer Counts

1	2	3	4	5	6	7	8	9	10	11	12	13	14	15	16
17	18	19	20	21	22	23	24	25	26	27	28	29	30	31	32

Drum Beats

1	2	3	4	5	6	7	8
9	10	11	12	13	14	15	16

EXAMPLE: Chapter 3, Lesson 3C: Dancing Fast and Slow Together

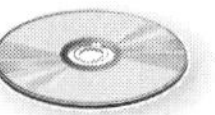

Alonzo King responded literally to the music in this section from *Dreamer.* The horns have a slow melody that is accompanied by a quick counterpoint in the strings. First the men move to the horns (adagio) and the women move to the strings (allegro), and then they switch so that the women move slowly and the men move quickly. The slow, steady melody provides a ground and stability for the wild, frenzied strings. The adagio movement is different from the allegro movement. Discuss the movement choices.

Improvisation 4: Sharing the Speed

- Divide into two groups again. The dancer half should dance their phrases while the audience claps the pulse. The performers move faster (double time) than the pulse.

• Switch roles and discuss the challenges of dancing quickly while moving in double time.

Problem Solving

Dancing Pulse Variations

• In groups of three, create a Contrasting Beat study. One dancer will dance the pulse, one will dance half time (slower), and one will dance double time (faster). Dancers will perform their phrases at the same time. Dancers already have nonlocomotor movement material in half time from improvisation 1, An Adagio, and locomotor movement material in double time from improvisation 3, An Allegro. The third dancer, the pulse, must find movement in a moderate tempo that will complement the other two movement phrases. All dancers should make adjustments to their choreography as needed. They do not have to dance their phrases exactly as before.

• The phrase should be 64 pulse beats long. The half-time and double-time dancers will adjust their phrases proportionately, each having their own dancer counts.

Dancer A (adagio, nonlocomotor movement)

______ ______ ______ ______ ______ ______ ______ ______

1 (2) 2 (2) 3 (2) 4 (2) 5 (2) 6 (2) 7 (2) 8 (2)

______ ______ ______ ______ ______ ______ ______ ______

9 (2) 10 (2) 11 (2) 12 (2) 13 (2) 14 (2) 15 (2) 16 (2)

Dancer B (pulse, any movement choice)

__ __ __ __ __ __ __ __ __ __ __ __ __ __ __ __

1 2 3 4 5 6 7 8 9 10 11 12 13 14 15 16

__ __ __ __ __ __ __ __ __ __ __ __ __ __ __ __

17 18 19 20 21 22 23 24 25 26 27 28 29 30 31 32

Dancer C (allegro, locomotor movement)

_ _

1 2 3 4 5 6 7 8 9 10 11 12 13 14 15 16 17 18 19 20 21 22 23 24 25 26 27 28 29 30 31 32

_ _

1 2 3 4 5 6 7 8 9 10 11 12 13 14 15 16 17 18 19 20 21 22 23 24 25 26 27 28 29 30 31 32

• Trios design a beginning shape and create pathways in space and on the floor that will allow the three phrases to relate to each other. Design an ending either with a shape or with an exit from the stage space.

Sharing the Pulse

• Each trio will perform their Contrasting Beat study. As they perform, the audience will clap the pulse beat for them.

• After each trio has performed, the teacher selects music with a clear pulse or a sound score to use as accompaniment. Each trio should perform its study again, this time accompanied by the chosen sound.

Discussion Questions

1. When might a choreographer use fast and slow movement together in the same movement sequence?
2. Are you always able to find the pulse or beat when listening to music? Can you find it as easily when dancing? Explain.
3. How do you usually find the underlying pulse in a piece of music?

Pacing: Combining Different Pulses

STATEMENT OF PERFORMANCE

Dancers will create a Contrasting Beat study with three dancers, demonstrating the pulse, the pulse in half time, and the pulse in double time.

Answer each of the following criteria with a yes or no and then score each category from 1 to 5, with 5 being the highest score and 1 the lowest. Use the rubrics to assist in discussion, self-reflection, and assessment of progress in understanding the choreographic concept.

Criteria	**Score**	
CREATING: PERCEPTUAL SKILLS	YES	NO
The dancers did the following:		
1. Made movement selections that clearly showed the different pulses.	_____	_____
2. Created three separate phrases.	_____	_____
3. Made spatial decisions that created unity in the composition so that the phrases could be performed at the same time.	_____	_____
Creating: Perceptual Skills Total	__________	
PERFORMING: TECHNICAL AND EXPRESSIVE SKILLS		
The dancers did the following:		
1. Accurately reproduced selected movement.	_____	_____
2. Moved clearly at the selected pace.	_____	_____
3. Flowed easily from one movement to the other.	_____	_____
4. Showed awareness of each other while performing.	_____	_____
Performing: Technical and Expressive Skills Total	__________	
RESPONDING: INTELLECTUAL AND REFLECTIVE SKILLS		
The dancers did the following:		
1. Discussed choices.	_____	_____
2. Made informed critical observations of own work.	_____	_____
3. Made informed critical observations of the work of others.	_____	_____
4. Noticed and discussed the similarities and differences in the different phrases.	_____	_____
Responding: Intellectual and Reflective Skills Total	__________	

SCORING

5 = Fulfilled all the criteria of creating, performing, and responding in a way that shows a thorough understanding of the skills and concepts to be mastered. Fully participated in the classroom tasks as a performer and as an audience member.

4 = Fulfilled all the criteria but does not yet show a thorough understanding of all skills and concepts. Fully participated in classroom tasks as a performer and as an audience member.

3 = Had difficulty fulfilling the criteria. Was not able to fully complete the assignment. Participated in class but could not complete all tasks as a performer and as an audience member.

2 = Did not complete the assigned work to a satisfactory degree. Did not fully participate as a performer or as an audience member.

1 = Did not participate.

ADDITIONAL COMMENTS

____

____

LESSON 4
ACCELERATING: HOW FAST CAN IT GO?

Introductory Statement

When speaking, we accelerate our words when we are excited or when we want to emphasize the content. Similarly, we slow down our speaking in order to clarify meaning or to soothe a young child. In music, acceleration is commonly used to heighten emotional response. A retard, or a gradual slowing, is often used at the end of a composition to prepare listeners for the resolution of the work. Gradual change of tempo, whether slow or fast, is another compositional device available to choreographers. It requires an understanding of movement timing and of the change in the amount of time it takes to perform the movement phrase.

Vocabulary

acceleration
beat
pulse
retard
tempo
unison

Warm-Up and Concept Introduction

• Listen to several pieces of music that are examples of accelerating the pulse, such as the following:

Edvard Grieg's "In the Hall of the Mountain King" from *Peer Gynt*
Reinhold Glière's "Dance of the Russian Sailors" from *The Red Poppy*
Arthur Honegger's *Pacific 231*

Uri Sands, the Impulse, pulls dancers Nicholle-Rochelle and Edgar Vardanian toward his center as he accelerates the pace of movement in this section of Dwight Rhoden's *Verge*.

• Listen to several pieces of music that feature retarding the pulse, such as the following:

Chopin's *Prelude in E Minor*

Puccini's "O Mio Babbino Cara," from *Gianni Schicchi*

Smetana's "The Moldau"

• Discuss what emotions are called forth by gradual tempo change in either direction.

- Begin a simple walking improvisation that changes tempo along with Grieg's "In the Hall of the Mountain King." Find the pulse and walk with it as it gradually gets faster.
- Choreograph a simple 16-count movement phrase that requires a level change. You might want to use one of the basic pulse movement phrases created in lesson 3 of this chapter. Set a pulse and dance the phrase with individual dancer counts. Repeat the phrase four times. Each time accelerate the phrase until during the fourth repetition the movement is quite fast. Discuss the challenges of accelerating a known phrase.
- Repeat the exercise. This time begin quickly and retard toward the end.

Structured Improvisations

Improvisation 1: Dance With the Pulse

Working alone, select and sequence movement for a 16-count phrase using any kind of movement. The movement should not be the same as the movement used in the warm-up. It should be completely new and combine locomotor and nonlocomotor movements. Each movement of the 16-count phrase should take only 1 count so that there are 16 movements to 16 beats.

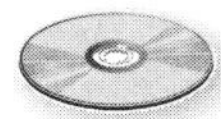

EXAMPLE: Chapter 3, Lesson 4A: Accelerating: How Fast Can It Go?

This section, "N'terole," from Alonzo King's *Chants*, is an example of acceleration in movement and music throughout a dance. Jeanene Russell begins the solo with large arm and leg extensions at a relatively slow pace. As the music repeats she begins to move more quickly with each repetition. At one point she begins her acceleration before the music, but in the next repetition the music clearly begins its acceleration and both dancer and music move faster and faster until she exits and the music fades away.

Improvisation 2: Gaining Speed

• Find a partner and share phrases. Now each pair has 32 counts to work with. Decide which phrase will be first and find a way to connect the two phrases so that there is a 32-count phrase for the two of you to perform in unison. In some cases, you may wish to rearrange a movement or two to make the movement flow better. The only stipulation for this duet is that you use all 32 movements (two 16-count phrases) to create one movement sequence.

• Next, add the compositional device of accelerating. Repeat the 32-count phrase twice, gradually increasing the speed of the performance until the sequence is as fast as it can go. Decide how slow the first phrase must be at the start in order to make the phrase move quicker and not make the last moments of the phrase impossible to perform. The teacher will provide a simple drum accompaniment to assist in increasing the speed.

- Decide on a beginning shape and an ending shape.

Improvisation 3: Checking the Speed

Perform the accelerating sequences as duets with the other dancers in class serving as the audience. Discuss how the movement changed when going faster.

Improvisation 4: Corner to Corner

From a designated corner and working with the same partner, create a locomotor movement phrase of whatever length necessary that shows one dancer chasing the other. Begin the phrase at one tempo, and as you move across the stage space accelerate the phrase with each repetition until exiting quickly. The tempo should be quite fast.

Problem Solving

Generating Speed

- With the same partner, create an Acceleration study that will use material from both previously-created phrases. Section A will include the 32-count phrase from improvisation 2, Gaining Speed, and section B will include the phrase of varying length from improvisation 4, Corner to Corner. Connect the two parts of the study and rehearse them so that they slowly accelerate. The last part, Corner to Corner, should end in a stage exit.
- Decide on an interesting and practical floor pathway for section B, the chase. Also, choose an interesting interpersonal spatial relationship for section A that may lead into the chase in section B. Motivation might be missing a bus, running late for a class, or avoiding an animal or insect.
- Decide where on stage to begin and end the first part of the study. Prepare a beginning shape. The study ends with the pair leaving the stage.

Acceleration Duets

Each duet will perform their Acceleration study. Accompaniment could be a simple drum beat that accelerates with the dancers, or there might be no accompaniment at all.

Discussion Questions

1. How does the performance of dance phrases change when they are accelerated?
2. What is your movement preference—do you prefer movement that is slower or faster?
3. What challenges did you meet when accelerating movement?

Accelerating: How Fast Can It Go?

STATEMENT OF PERFORMANCE

In duets, dancers will create an Acceleration study that consists of a 32-count movement phrase (section A) and a "chasing" locomotor sequence (section B) that will be performed while continually moving faster and faster until exiting the performing space.

Answer each of the following criteria with a yes or no and then score each category from 1 to 5, with 5 being the highest score and 1 the lowest. Use the rubrics to assist in discussion, self-reflection, and assessment of progress in understanding the choreographic concept.

Criteria	Score	
CREATING: PERCEPTUAL SKILLS	YES	NO
The dancer did the following:		
1. Made good choices in timing and transitions.	_____	_____
2. Followed the assignment accurately.	_____	_____
3. Collaborated with a partner to make a 32-count movement phrase (A).	_____	_____
4. Collaborated with a partner to create a "chasing" phrase (B).	_____	_____
5. Used acceleration correctly as a compositional device.	_____	_____
Creating: Perceptual Skills Total	__________	
PERFORMING: TECHNICAL AND EXPRESSIVE SKILLS		
The dancer did the following:		
1. Accurately reproduced selected movement.	_____	_____
2. Remembered both dance sections.	_____	_____
3. Flowed easily from one movement to the other.	_____	_____
4. Gradually accelerated selected movement.	_____	_____
Performing: Technical and Expressive Skills Total	__________	
RESPONDING: INTELLECTUAL AND REFLECTIVE SKILLS		
The dancer did the following:		
1. Discussed choices.	_____	_____
2. Made informed critical observations of own work.	_____	_____
3. Made informed critical observations of the work of others.	_____	_____
4. Identified tempo differences.	_____	_____
Responding: Intellectual and Reflective Skills Total	__________	

SCORING

5 = Fulfilled all the criteria of creating, performing, and responding in a way that shows a thorough understanding of the skills and concepts to be mastered. Fully participated in the classroom tasks as a performer and as an audience member.

4 = Fulfilled all the criteria but does not yet show a thorough understanding of all skills and concepts. Fully participated in classroom tasks as a performer and as an audience member.

3 = Had difficulty fulfilling the criteria. Was not able to fully complete the assignment. Participated in class but could not complete all tasks as a performer and as an audience member.

2 = Did not complete the assigned work to a satisfactory degree. Did not fully participate as a performer or as an audience member.

1 = Did not participate.

ADDITIONAL COMMENTS

____

____

LESSON 5
PROBLEM SOLVING: CREATING A TRIO

© Rolland Elliott

Edgar Vardanian, Nicholle-Rochelle, and Uri Sands dance a trio from *Verge* that features variations in tempo.

Introductory Statement

In the previous four lessons, structured improvisations led to short movement studies based on dance concepts associated with time. The previous lessons dealt with slow or adagio movement and its contrast, allegro or fast movement. In the third lesson, dancers created studies that combined slow and fast movement against a steady pulse. In the fourth lesson, the concept of accelerating movement was explored. The expressive potential of tempo in dance provides the choreographer with yet another tool for dance composition. In order to solve the creative problem of this lesson, choreographers must identify a theme or central idea that can be expressed through changes of tempo.

Creating a Trio

EXAMPLE: Chapter 3, Lesson 5A: Trio From *Chants*

In this trio from *Chants,* Kati Hanlon Mayo and Traci Gilchrest move across the stage dancing the same movements but in their own timing, taking liberties with the pulse as they wish. The music clearly establishes the pulse so the dancers can improvise with the timing. Behind them, Hernan Justo dances in half time until he reaches the end of the stage and moves to the pulse.

In this final assignment based on the concept of time, three dancers will work together to create the assigned composition (see figure 3.2). In the previous studies of this chapter, dancers have created phrases of adagio movement and allegro movement, have danced different pulse speeds at the same time, and have explored accelerating or retarding movement phrases. The challenge inherent in this study is finding a theme that can sustain a dance composition of 3 to 5 minutes.

Each composition should clearly show tempo changes between sections; a point or several points of acceleration; and one section that features the dancers showing the pulse, its half time, and its double time all performed together.

A Tempo Trio

As an example, make a list of actions and discuss the tempo that might represent these images. Then create new situations or emotions that might represent changes of tempo in movement.

Anger, to resolution, to calmness

Calmness, to confrontation, to anger

Inertia, to chaos, to balance

A turtle, a bear, and a hummingbird

A haunted house requiring one to enter slowly, overcome several fearful surprises, only to leave as quickly as possible by the rear door when frightened again

FIGURE 3.2 Use these examples to get started on your own trio.

Choosing the Sound

Ideally, a musician will improvise sound to accompany the studies. Dancers should assume the responsibility of telling the musician how they are counting their study with dancer counts so that the musician can create a suitable sound environment.

If a musician is not available, listen to a variety of music that has a clear, steady beat so that dancers can dance the pulse, half time, and double time.

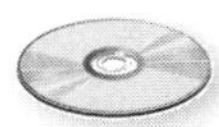

EXAMPLE: Chapter 3, Lesson 5B: Trio From *Verge*

In this trio from *Verge,* the dancers have a strong musical pulse to guide them. This short segment shows Uri Sands as the Impulse moving slowly in place while his alter ego, Edgar Vardanian, and his partner, Mia Cunningham, move on the pulse and in double time. They show the pulse in different body parts. Watch the three interpretations of the beat.

Problem Solving: Creating a Trio

STATEMENT OF PERFORMANCE

Dancers will create and perform a tempo trio based on the movement material explored in the lessons in chapter 3.

Answer each of the following criteria with a yes or no and then score each category from 1 to 5, with 5 being the highest score and 1 the lowest. Use the rubrics to assist in discussion, self-reflection, and assessment of progress in understanding the choreographic concept.

Criteria	**Score**	
CREATING: PERCEPTUAL SKILLS	YES	NO
The dancers did the following:		
1. Selected and developed movement material generated in previous four lessons.	_____	_____
2. Selected an appropriate guiding theme.	_____	_____
3. Found creative solutions for order and movement material selected.	_____	_____
4. Included slow and fast tempo changes and acceleration.	_____	_____
5. Danced different tempos together.	_____	_____
6. Collaborated with two other dancers to make movement choices.	_____	_____
Creating: Perceptual Skills Total	___________	
PERFORMING: TECHNICAL AND EXPRESSIVE SKILLS		
The dancers did the following:		
1. Accurately reproduced selected movement.	_____	_____
2. Flowed easily from one movement to another.	_____	_____
3. Successfully performed acceleration in movement.	_____	_____
Performing: Technical and Expressive Skills Total	___________	
RESPONDING: INTELLECTUAL AND REFLECTIVE SKILLS		
The dancers did the following:		
1. Discussed choices.	_____	_____
2. Made informed critical observations of own work.	_____	_____
3. Made informed critical observations of the work of others.	_____	_____
Responding: Intellectual and Reflective Skills Total	___________	

SCORING

5 = Fulfilled all the criteria of creating, performing, and responding in a way that shows a thorough understanding of the skills and concepts to be mastered. Fully participated in the classroom tasks as a performer and as an audience member.

4 = Fulfilled all the criteria but does not yet show a thorough understanding of all skills and concepts. Fully participated in classroom tasks as a performer and as an audience member.

3 = Had difficulty fulfilling the criteria. Was not able to fully complete the assignment. Participated in class but could not complete all tasks as a performer and as an audience member.

2 = Did not complete the assigned work to a satisfactory degree. Did not fully participate as a performer or as an audience member.

1 = Did not participate.

ADDITIONAL COMMENTS

____

____

Student Self-Evaluation Questions

Name: ______________________ Date: ____________ Class: ____________

CREATIVE ASSIGNMENT

1. What were the most interesting tempo changes you and your partners made?

2. What was the most challenging problem you had to solve while you were working together with tempo changes?

3. How did you solve the creative problem together? Describe the process.

4. What did you learn about yourself as a collaborator while you were trying to solve the problem?

5. What was the role of improvisation in generating material for your study?

6. How did you decide on the structure for your dance?

7. What is another project or experience that might grow out of this one?

Chapter 4

Energy: Force Generating Movement

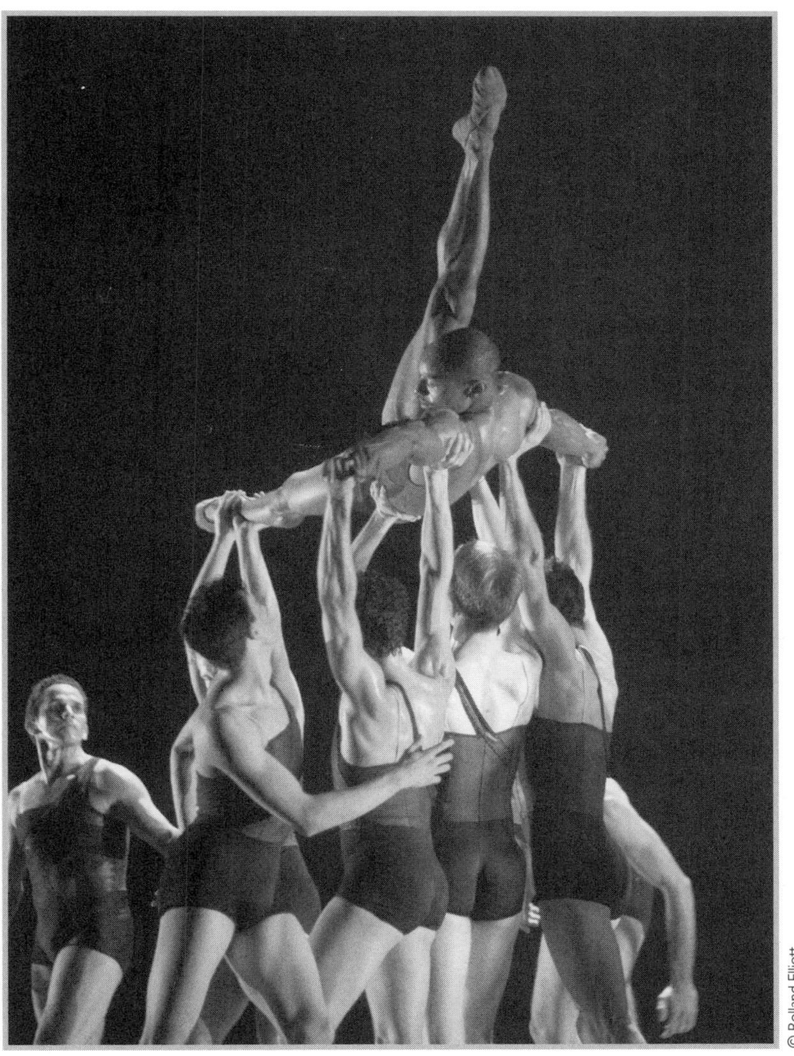

In an important emotional moment from Dwight Rhoden's *Verge*, the Impulse character is raised high over the heads of the other dancers with great intensity. The shape evokes energy. The Impulse character is supported and moved by the whole group.

OVERVIEW

Energy is a word used to describe the force behind movement. In dance it refers to the dynamic qualities in a choreographed phrase or the effort needed to produce a given movement. Alonzo King refers to it as the "texture in between." Terms such as *sudden, sustained, strong, light, vibratory, suspended, swing,* and *collapse* are common dance vocabulary words used to describe energy qualities.

Energy may be shown through different stages of movement intensity. The amount of energy used to produce a movement may be light and soft or strong and intense. Also, the speed of a movement requires different kinds of energy. If someone is moving quickly and strongly, different energy expenditure is required from that of someone moving slowly and lightly.

To Alonzo King, movement isn't a decoration. It's not a pose. It's an action the dancer responds to. Movement speaks to the dancer and creates emotional states that are reflected in the actions of a dance work. The audience responds empathetically to the actions of the dancers as they perform the movement with clarity and emotional intensity. The conscious use of energy behind movement provides dance phrases with additional shadings of meaning and dimension.

Energy is the texture in between movement. Movements speak to the dancers. Physical states create emotional states.

ALONZO KING, 1999

© Mitchell Kearney

Shell Bauman and Mia Cunningham depict an emotional moment from Alonzo King's *Map.* Her body position and seeming lack of energy in opposition to his straightforward gaze and wrapping gestures show two dancers with entirely different qualities of movement dancing at the same time.

In this chapter, the dynamics of movement are explored. The chapter begins with gravity in weight-sharing explorations and proceeds to different uses of weight and force progressing from light to strong, from slow to fast. The culminating activity involves the creation of an original quartet that grows in intensity from slow and sustained to fast and sudden and back again to slow and sustained movement.

LESSON 1
INERTIA: READINESS TO MOVE

Introductory Statement

Gravity is a force that binds us to the earth. If we allow ourselves to passively give into that force, we feel heavy and have difficulty moving. Our center lowers and we drop our weight into the lower half of the body. As we take this feeling of weight and move with it, gravity gives strength and power to the movement. During the 20th century the use of weight both actively and passively became an important element in dance training and choreography.

Vocabulary

active weight
heaviness
inertia
passive weight
sustained movement

EXAMPLE: Chapter 4, Lesson 1A: Weight and Heaviness

In this example, we see Alonzo King creating the movement for Tamas (inertia or ignorance). The movement of the character is heavy and passive. The group must move the character forward. The character cannot move without the support and manipulation of the group.

Warm-Up and Concept Introduction

• Begin a simple walk around the general space. Start to give in to gravity so that there is a sense of weight in the pelvis, a heaviness in the gait that is expressed by the use of the *plié* or softening of the knees. Return to normal walking and gradually begin to raise the weight center to the rib cage. Rise to the toes and sense the feeling of lightness. Return to normal walking.

• In pairs, participate in an active and passive improvisation where one partner, the active leader, completely moves the passive partner. The passive partner lies down on the floor with eyes closed. The active partner selects an arm, a leg, or the head and picks it up slowly or simply holds it, moving it gently. The passive partner should offer no assistance. Explore different ways the chosen body part can move. Note the weight and range of motion, especially of the leg. The active partner should find ways to support the different joints in each extremity as they move. Carefully place the body part back on the floor and take another. Try three or four different extremities and then exchange roles.

• Explore locomotor movement with your partner. The active partner should pick up a leg and place it in one direction, then pick up the other leg. The passive partner should offer no help. The active partner may try to push a foot to move the passive partner forward.

EXAMPLE: Chapter 4, Lesson 1B: Moving Weight

Watch as a group of dancers negotiate how to move the passive weight of the character Tamas forward, as Tamas stands and is completely supported by her partners. Note how Alonzo King tries out the movement himself to feel the quality before he watches the dancers.

- Try rolling each other on the ground in several different ways, always maintaining an active and passive partner.
- The active partner should try to push the passive partner across the floor, from the pelvis. Partners probably will not move much as it is hard to push someone into space, but the effort and strength required to move a heavy weight will be experienced.

Structured Improvisations

Improvisation 1: Inertia-Shaping Weight

- Working in trios, let one member be completely passive. The other two active dancers begin forming the inert, heavy person into shapes by moving different body parts, one after the other. One dancer will have to support the passive weight by holding, bracing, or balancing the weighted dancer while the third dancer moves the heavy body parts. In other words, the trio consists of the weight (dancer A), the support (dancer B), and the mover (dancer C). Exchange roles so everyone in the group can experience being the weight.

EXAMPLE: Chapter 4, Lesson 1C: Moving Shapes

Watch the active dancers move the legs and arms of Tamas into varied shapes. Watch how continuous and sustained the movement looks. Tamas is completely dependent on the group for her movement.

- Find ways to travel with the passive person into space, always working together so that every move uses some form of weight sharing. Use lifts and counterbalances to create a slow, weighted locomotor sequence of movement.

Problem Solving

EXAMPLE: Chapter 4, Lesson 1D: Inertia Dances

Amy Earnest portrays the character Tamas in the ballet *Dreamer* by Alonzo King. In this excerpt we see her first entrance as the group coaxes her into movement and action. They support her passive weight, move her feet and push her forward, and shape her legs and arms. Note the sustained, heavy quality created by this use of passive weight.

Overcoming Inertia

Continue to work in trios to create an Inertia study:

a. Compose four balanced weight-sharing shapes. Each shape contains one dancer as weight, one dancer as support, and one dancer as mover. In the four shapes, roles may change as independent transitions are prepared between each shape.

b. Find a way to walk with one passive member to a new place in space. The active members of the trio should pick up the feet of the passive dancer, roll the dancer, or push the dancer through space however they can. The passive dancer may be lying, seated, or standing.

c. Manipulate the extremities of the passive dancer, creating sustained movements and unusual shapes. Shape the weight. Both active dancers move separate body parts of the passive dancer at the same time.

d. Compose a final movement during which the two active dancers lift the passive dancer off the ground and hold the weight in stillness.

Sharing the Experience

Perform the studies for other trios. Each trio should select a sound score, such as the recording of rainforest sounds, birdcalls, or traffic in a city, to accompany the study.

Discussion Questions

1. How would you define weight?
2. Define gravity. How do we specifically refer to and use it in dance?
3. How does it feel to be supported by someone? What allows you to trust a partner enough to give him your weight?
4. What might be a reason for a choreographer to use weight sharing in a dance work?

Inertia: Readiness to Move

STATEMENT OF PERFORMANCE

In trios, dancers will create and perform an Inertia study based on heaviness. The study explores balancing weight, lifting weight, moving weight, and shaping weight, emphasizing sustained movement transitions between each movement.

Answer each of the following criteria with a yes or no and then score each category from 1 to 5, with 5 being the highest score and 1 the lowest. Use the rubrics to assist in discussion, self-reflection, and assessment of progress in understanding the choreographic concept.

Criteria	**Score** YES	NO
CREATING: PERCEPTUAL SKILLS The dancers did the following:		
1. Made clear, slow, sustained movement selections.	_____	_____
2. Created four body shapes, manipulating passive weight.	_____	_____
3. Moved through space, guiding a passive partner.	_____	_____
4. Explored lifting, carrying, and shaping weight.	_____	_____
5. Found an interdependent ending shape.	_____	_____
Creating: Perceptual Skills Total	__________	
PERFORMING: TECHNICAL AND EXPRESSIVE SKILLS The dancers did the following:		
1. Accurately reproduced selected movement.	_____	_____
2. Demonstrated sustained movement throughout.	_____	_____
3. Flowed easily from one action to the other.	_____	_____
4. Exhibited active and passive weight.	_____	_____
Performing: Technical and Expressive Skills Total	__________	
RESPONDING: INTELLECTUAL AND REFLECTIVE SKILLS The dancers did the following:		
1. Discussed choices.	_____	_____
2. Made informed critical observations of own work.	_____	_____
3. Made informed critical observations of the work of others.	_____	_____
4. Noticed and discussed the similarities and differences in the different phrases.	_____	_____
Responding: Intellectual and Reflective Skills Total	__________	

SCORING

5 = Fulfilled all the criteria of creating, performing, and responding in a way that shows a thorough understanding of the skills and concepts to be mastered. Fully participated in the classroom tasks as a performer and as an audience member.

4 = Fulfilled all the criteria but does not yet show a thorough understanding of all skills and concepts. Fully participated in classroom tasks as a performer and as an audience member.

3 = Had difficulty fulfilling the criteria. Was not able to fully complete the assignment. Participated in class but could not complete all tasks as a performer and as an audience member.

2 = Did not complete the assigned work to a satisfactory degree. Did not fully participate as a performer or as an audience member.

1 = Did not participate.

ADDITIONAL COMMENTS

____

____

LESSON 2
OPPOSITES: CONTRASTING ENERGIES

© Rolland Elliott

In this picture of the final movement from *Verge*, we see three dancers demonstrating contrasting energy. Jason Jacobs explodes through the air while Mia Cunningham rests heavily on Alex Donovan, who supports her in a strong, solid stance.

Vocabulary

contract (close)
expand (open)
fall
force
formation
gravity
light
rise
sink
strong

Introductory Statement

In the previous lesson, we explored how the force of gravity pulls the body downward, which produces a feeling of heaviness. In most dance movements, we wish to use gravity actively and we pull away from it in order to remain in an upright position, or locomote through space, or jump into the air. In this lesson, we explore the ebb and flow of energy throughout the body with opposite amounts of force in movement. Dancers will explore strong and light movement along with the concepts of expanding and contracting, opening and closing, and rising and sinking.

Warm-Up and Exploring Contrasts

• Walk normally throughout the space in a moderate tempo. Actively focus attention on the pelvis and drop the weight downward so that your steps are weighted and make a definite sound as they hit the floor. The legs begin to bend and eventually the movement remains in a low walk.

• Lift the weight out of the pelvis and into the rib cage so that the center of the body lifts and the steps become lighter. You might even rise to the toes.

• Find a natural walking preference once again and repeat the exercise several times until you understand and can demonstrate the active shift of weight between lightness and strength.

Expanding and Contracting

EXAMPLE: Chapter 4, Lesson 2A: Defining Opening and Closing

Alonzo King is rehearsing the dancers in *Dreamer,* looking for a specific sustained quality in movements that are closing and opening. He wants movement, not positions. Watch the torsos of the dancers as they incorporate texture into their movement.

• Begin a structured improvisation using the action words *open, close, rise,* and *sink.* Expand as wide as possible for every opening and contract as small as possible for every closing. Rise to as expanded a position as possible and sink into as contracted a position as possible. The weight of the body is now used actively to change the quality of the movement as it expands into the periphery in lightness or contracts back into the body with a strong inward pull.

• Find four different ways to show expansion and contraction related to rising, falling, opening, and closing. Try to use different body parts as small as the hand as well as whole-body movement. Explore moving through all three levels in space: high, middle, and low.

Describing the Flow

Discuss word pairs that come to mind as the exercise progresses, such as the following:

Grow and shrink
Intensify and weaken
Wax and wane
Advance and retreat
Rise and fall
Open and close
Expand and contract
Push and pull
Gather and strew

Structured Improvisations

Improvisation 1: Exploring Time With Intensity

• As we pull away from gravity, we naturally move more slowly than when we give in to gravity. We rise more slowly than we sink. In dance, however, we often choose the opposite energy and we rise quickly and sink slowly. In the last exercise, each dancer created four different ways to show expansion and contraction. Now assign counts to each action word. Rising movements should take 6 counts and sinking movements should take 2 counts. Opening should take 6 counts and closing should take 2 counts. Following that improvisation, do the reverse—all risings and openings should be 2 counts and all sinkings and closings should be 6 counts. Finally, try the same sequence with each action performed in 4 counts so that they all receive an equal amount of time.

- Note how gravity is used in this exercise. Where is lightness? Where is strength? Do we usually expand into lightness and contract with strength? How does it feel to do the opposite? Could we ever choose to expand with strength and contract with lightness? For each phrase choose either lightness or strength.
- Observe each others' performances. Discuss what you observed as an audience and what you experienced while moving.

Improvisation 2: Expanding Space

- Working in trios, face one another. The interpersonal space between each trio becomes important and is defined by the body placement of the dancers, or the formation. Find a starting shape using all three dancers. Explore how to make the space between you expand and contract. The shape itself may expand and contract, leading the dancers to move away from (retreat) and move toward (advance) each other by using simple locomotor movement. Find four different ways to expand into space away from each other only to be followed by a contraction back, each time returning to the same starting point. Do you feel any natural tendencies, such as retreating quickly or advancing slowly? Try several tempo variations.
- As you move away from each other quickly, move into lightness, only to change into strength as you advance more slowly toward each other.

Problem Solving

EXAMPLE: Chapter 4, Lesson 2B: Trio of Gunas

In Alonzo King's *Dreamer,* the three gunas, or characteristics of existence, are the first dancers to appear on the stage. They enter from different parts of the stage and advance toward each other to meet in the center of the stage. Their movement expands and contracts like breathing, as if they are summoning their energies to assist the birth of a new life.

Give and Take

Continuing in trios, work cooperatively to create a Give and Take study. The study should include the following:

a. A beginning trio shape.

b. Section A: Expand the shape between the three of you and contract to a new shape in four different ways using levels and nonlocomotor movements. Assign counts to each opening and closing so that each has a different count pattern that adds up to 8, such as 5 counts to open followed by 3 counts to close, 2 counts to open followed by 6 counts to close, and so on. This section should be 32 counts divided into four 8s.

c. Section B: Retreat into space away from each other and advance back toward each other four times. Each repetition should move out farther into space until the final expansion catapults everyone completely offstage, which will end the study. Each repetition should have a different combination of locomotor movements with different tempos and count structures for each retreat and advance. Do not be limited by groupings of 8. Try dividing 10 counts or 6 counts.

Sharing the Experience

Perform the studies for each other without music, listening only to the breath of the dancers.

Discussion Questions

1. Do we usually expand into lightness and contract with strength? Explain.
2. How does it feel to use strength as we expand into space and lightness to contract back into ourselves?
3. How do the concepts of rising, falling, opening, closing, advancing, and retreating relate to three-dimensionality?

Opposites: Contrasting Energies

STATEMENT OF PERFORMANCE

In trios, dancers will create and perform a Give and Take study that demonstrates movement that expands and contracts using strong and light energy with locomotor and nonlocomotor movement.

Answer each of the following criteria with a yes or no and then score each category from 1 to 5, with 5 being the highest score and 1 the lowest. Use the rubrics to assist in discussion, self-reflection, and assessment of progress in understanding the choreographic concept.

Criteria	Score	
CREATING: PERCEPTUAL SKILLS The dancers did the following:	YES	NO
1. Created four nonlocomotor movement phrases expanding and contracting into space.	_____	_____
2. Created four locomotor movement phrases expanding and contracting into space.	_____	_____
3. Showed use of strong and light energy.	_____	_____
4. Used a different count structure for each phrase.	_____	_____
Creating: Perceptual Skills Total	__________	
PERFORMING: TECHNICAL AND EXPRESSIVE SKILLS The dancers did the following:		
1. Accurately reproduced selected movement.	_____	_____
2. Demonstrated expanded and contracted movement.	_____	_____
3. Flowed from one movement to another with ease.	_____	_____
Performing: Technical and Expressive Skills Total	__________	
RESPONDING: INTELLECTUAL AND REFLECTIVE SKILLS The dancers did the following:		
1. Discussed choices.	_____	_____
2. Made informed critical observations of own work.	_____	_____
3. Made informed critical observations of the work of others.	_____	_____
4. Noticed and discussed the similarities and differences in the different phrases.	_____	_____
Responding: Intellectual and Reflective Skills Total	__________	

SCORING

5 = Fulfilled all the criteria of creating, performing, and responding in a way that shows a thorough understanding of the skills and concepts to be mastered. Fully participated in the classroom tasks as a performer and as an audience member.

4 = Fulfilled all the criteria but does not yet show a thorough understanding of all skills and concepts. Fully participated in classroom tasks as a performer and as an audience member.

3 = Had difficulty fulfilling the criteria. Was not able to fully complete the assignment. Participated in class but could not complete all tasks as a performer and as an audience member.

2 = Did not complete the assigned work to a satisfactory degree. Did not fully participate as a performer or as an audience member.

1 = Did not participate.

ADDITIONAL COMMENTS

____

____

LESSON 3
DYNAMICS: QUALITIES OF MOVEMENT

Vocabulary

collapsed
dynamic qualities
dynamics
energy
percussive
suspended
sustained
swinging
vibratory

Introductory Statement

The use of different gradations of energy to perform a movement is often described as adding dynamic quality to movement. Specifically, in dance we identify six dynamic qualities: sustained, percussive, swinging, suspended, collapsed, and vibratory.

Sustained = slow, smooth, continuous, even
Percussive = sudden, sharp, choppy, jagged
Swinging = sway, to and fro, pendulum, undercurve
Suspended = stillness, balance, high point
Collapsed = fall, release, relax
Vibratory = shake, tremble, wiggle

© Rolland Elliott

Uri Sands, the Impulse, is suspended high above the ground after executing a strong percussive jump. The other dancers collapse and sink under him in curved shapes.

Warm-Up and Quality Definitions

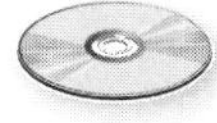

EXAMPLE: Chapter 4, Lesson 3A: Describing a Quality

Alonzo King wanted specific dynamic qualities expressed in movement while choreographing *Dreamer.* In this example, watch King describe and demonstrate a percussive movement phrase and the dancers show percussiveness in their bodies.

Warm up by moving within each quality:

Swinging (using legs, then arms, then whole body)

Collapsed (swing a leg up, then collapse the body over it; repeat, alternating legs)

Sustained (melt gradually all the way to the floor until finishing in a stretched shape)

Percussive (rise quickly and begin a rhythmic step-clap-stamp phrase)

Suspended (rise to relevé on both feet and allow arms to follow; find a point of balance, balance on one foot)

Vibratory (begin a soft beating of the feet on the floor and allow the vibration to move up through the body like a volcano until it erupts out through the fingers)

Structured Improvisations

Sample Locomotor and Nonlocomotor Sequence

Swinging legs with forward steps
Sustained arm stretch
Percussive jumps
Vibratory beating
Collapsing low walk
Suspended breathing

FIGURE 4.1 Dynamic qualities using both locomotor and nonlocomotor movement.

Improvisation 1: Moving Energy

Using a simple walk, explore moving through space using the dynamic qualities (see figure 4.1). Discuss how the walk changes when a specific dynamic motivates the movement. How does the tempo alter with each quality? Which qualities can be performed with light energy? Which ones require strength?

EXAMPLE: Chapter 4, Lesson 3B: Sustained Movement

In this excerpt, Alonzo King works with dancer Amy Earnest to create slow, sustained movement for a section of *Dreamer.*

Improvisation 2: Sharing Qualities

- Divide into two groups. Half will dance, half will be the audience. One member of the audience will call out a dynamic quality. The dancers will move in general space in the quality that is called out. Continue in one quality until another is called out randomly. Call out in unexpected ways, slowly and quickly. Explore each quality with both nonlocomotor and locomotor movement.
- Exchange roles until everyone has improvised movement phrases in each quality, quickly changing qualities as they are called out.
- Discuss feelings or emotions that are implied by the different movement qualities and list them on a chart (see figure 4.2).

Movement Qualities

Swinging legs—regularity, evenness
Sustained, stretched arms—laziness, calm
Percussive jumps—happiness, joy, excitement
Vibratory beating—anger, resentment
Collapsing walks—defeat, failure, grief
Suspended breath—anticipation, surprise

FIGURE 4.2 Sample feelings and emotions implied by the movement qualities.

Problem Solving

- In a hat, place slips of paper with one dynamic quality written on each piece. Draw one slip of paper from the hat and find two other partners to make a trio. Together look at the three slips of paper. The problem is to create a Dynamic Quality study using only the three qualities selected. The challenge is to find a way to transition between the qualities in a convincing way so that the study is cohesive. The study should be at least 1 minute long. The study should have a clear beginning and ending shape and use both locomotor and nonlocomotor movements.
- Perform the Dynamic Quality studies for each other. Audience members should identify the dynamic qualities chosen. Discuss how it feels to spend a specific amount of time in only one movement quality. Do we do this in natural movement?

Discussion Questions

1. In your own words, define *energy.* Find your own definitions for each of the dynamic qualities.
2. When might you move naturally in a percussive way?
3. Do emotional states affect how we use energy in movement?
4. List different action words that could describe each of the six qualities.

Dynamics: Qualities of Movement

STATEMENT OF PERFORMANCE

In trios, dancers will create a Dynamic Quality study of approximately 1 minute in length using three dynamic qualities selected at random.

Answer each of the following criteria with a yes or no and then score each category from 1 to 5, with 5 being the highest score and 1 the lowest. Use the rubrics to assist in discussion, self-reflection, and assessment of progress in understanding the choreographic concept.

Criteria	Score YES	NO
CREATING: PERCEPTUAL SKILLS The dancers did the following:		
1. Made three clear dynamic quality changes.	_____	_____
2. Used locomotor and nonlocomotor movement.	_____	_____
3. Contributed movement ideas.	_____	_____
Creating: Perceptual Skills Total	__________	
PERFORMING: TECHNICAL AND EXPRESSIVE SKILLS The dancers did the following:		
1. Accurately reproduced selected movement.	_____	_____
2. Demonstrated clear quality changes.	_____	_____
3. Flowed easily from one movement quality to another.	_____	_____
Performing: Technical and Expressive Skills Total	__________	
RESPONDING: INTELLECTUAL AND REFLECTIVE SKILLS The dancers did the following:		
1. Discussed choices.	_____	_____
2. Made informed critical observations of own work.	_____	_____
3. Made informed critical observations of the work of others.	_____	_____
4. Noticed and discussed the similarities and differences in the different phrases.	_____	_____
Responding: Intellectual and Reflective Skills Total	__________	

SCORING

5 = Fulfilled all the criteria of creating, performing, and responding in a way that shows a thorough understanding of the skills and concepts to be mastered. Fully participated in the classroom tasks as a performer and as an audience member.

4 = Fulfilled all the criteria but does not yet show a thorough understanding of all skills and concepts. Fully participated in classroom tasks as a performer and as an audience member.

3 = Had difficulty fulfilling the criteria. Was not able to fully complete the assignment. Participated in class but could not complete all tasks as a performer and as an audience member.

2 = Did not complete the assigned work to a satisfactory degree. Did not fully participate as a performer or as an audience member.

1 = Did not participate.

ADDITIONAL COMMENTS

____

____

____

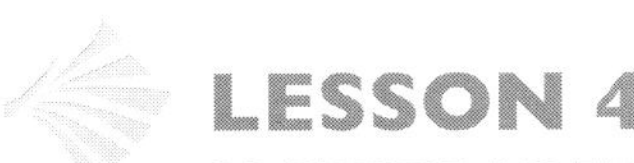

LESSON 4
INTENSITY: INCREASING AND DECREASING FORCE

Vocabulary

dynamic qualities
intensity
tempo

Introductory Statement

In chapter 3, lesson 4, dancers created a study that built dramatic intensity by accelerating the tempo from slow to fast. In this lesson, dancers will explore how to build dramatic intensity by using dynamic qualities. Often intensity on stage is achieved by adding more movement or more force behind each movement. Intensity is also achieved by adding more dancers to the stage, generating more force by accumulating more bodies to perform the actions. Whether we use tempo acceleration, dynamic intensity change, or the addition of dancers, the desire is the same: to evoke a strong emotional response in the viewer.

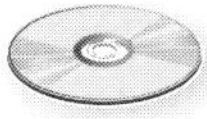

EXAMPLE: Chapter 4, Lesson 4A: Demonstrating Intensity

Alonzo King introduces the concept of energy in movement by demonstrating intensity, or the passive and active use of weight. Intensity can be low, completely giving into gravity; medium, with a combination of strength and passivity; or high, using weight actively and strongly.

In the same way, in music emotional intensity and sound expansion and contraction are produced by adding more instruments or by playing the instruments softly or loudly. Play a musical example of a gradual growth in intensity that is

© Rolland Elliot

A cast of 15 dancers on stage at the same time, doing the same action percussively and moving along the same pathway, builds a certain intensity of emotion. In this last section from Dwight Rhoden's *Verge*, the dancers move closer and closer to the center of the target, moving quickly in unison to build intensity and anticipation.

created by loudness versus softness, such as Ravel's *Bolero*. Note if there is a gradual addition of musical instruments as well.

Warm-Up and Exploring Intensity

- Build a movement phrase beginning with slow and sustained movement in one body part. Gradually move it with more force and speed and accumulate other body parts until the whole body is moving strongly and percussively. Gradually decrease the intensity by removing one body part at a time until you are still.
- Begin slowly with sustained movement and gradually build up to a percussive, vibratory movement until the energy explodes or collapses quickly.
- Discuss the emotional difference between the two phrases. Do both have the same high points? If you were to draw both phrases what might each drawing look like? Where would the thickest lines be?

Structured Improvisations

Improvisation 1: Intensity Grows Into Space

Start from low-intensity movement in one body part and gradually add more movement and other parts of the body with stronger qualities and a quicker tempo until the energy explodes and collapses such as was danced in the warm-up. Decide what body parts will be added, and when, so that everyone makes the same choices. Think about the movement growing from smaller to larger in space as well as with intensity, and keep in mind that all dancers will be moving the same body parts at the same time. See the following sample sequence.

- **Section 1.** Find a standing shape that uses curves in the torso. The arms and head should be collapsed and at rest. Gently begin to lift the head and slowly move just the arms, drawing straight and curved lines in space. Moving nothing but the arms, draw air pathways all over your personal space. Movement should be slow and sustained.

EXAMPLE: Chapter 4, Lesson 4B: Soft, Sustained Arms

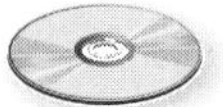

In this example, Alonzo King created soft and sustained movement for the head and arms.

- **Section 2.** Catch one foot with a hand and begin to move the foot and hand as if glued together. Explore different ways to move with one foot and one hand connected. Explore turning, changing direction, and changing hands, but remain always with one hand in contact with one foot. Change arms and feet to explore a new point of connectedness between two body parts. Movement will be sustained and swinging and may often be suspended.

EXAMPLE: Chapter 4, Lesson 4C: Arms and Legs

Dancers explore ways to move a connected arm and leg around the body while using sustained movement.

• **Section 3.** Release the foot and begin to find larger, expansive movements that the now-released arms and legs can do together. Explore circles, figure eights, high levels, low levels, and especially turns, using arms and legs moving together. Begin to increase the intensity of the energy and expand into space with the gestures as if awakening from sleep or breaking out of a shell. The dynamics should move from swinging to percussive as the intensity grows. The exploration should remain in personal space.

EXAMPLE: Chapter 4, Lesson 4D: Leg and Arm Circles With Jumps

Watch the dancers explore circular space as their movements grow in intensity and assume a percussive and sometimes vibratory quality.

• **Section 4.** Begin to move arms and legs faster. Jumps explode percussively into the air at least four times. Keep the arms and legs moving in between jumps while using shaking or vibratory movements.

• **Section 5.** After completing the four jumps, collapse one body part at a time until ending in a crumpled shape on a low level. After completing the phrase, discuss how it felt.

Improvisation 2: Watching It Grow

• Divide into two groups. With a cue to start, the first group will dance through their sequences in their own time, simply waiting in their ending shape until all have finished. Discuss how the dynamics of the movement added an emotional buildup as the movement energy increased. What was the most exciting moment of the improvisation?

• Repeat the exercise with the second half of the group.

Problem Solving

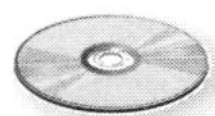

EXAMPLE: Chapter 4, Lesson 4E: An Energy Continuum

In this sequence from Alonzo King's *Dreamer*, watch the whole room grow in energy and intensity. All the dancers follow the same movement instructions but have individual movements and timings. As the stage grows in intensity, watch the dynamic qualities change. Finally, watch all the energy dissipate as the dancers collapse to the floor.

Energy in Action

• Discuss the concept of growing and the stages of development in humans and animals. What are the stages we pass through while growing? How could these stages be shown in movement? Discuss the concept of metamorphosis from a caterpillar (slow, crawling on the ground) to a butterfly (quick and flying), or from an infant to a child (from lying to sitting to crawling to standing still to walking to running). Each is a gradual buildup of strength and control of energy to a high point followed by some sort of resolution.

• In groups of six or more, with one dancer serving both as choreographer and as dancer, create an Energy study that uses new movement material. Find an original theme to help generate new movement and shapes. Design a formation for the whole group. Everyone will begin together and follow individual timing for the selected movement. The choreographer should step back to observe how the sequence is developing and offer suggestions to keep the group cohesive and the intensity building. The study should have five different sections and use at least five of the movement qualities.

Sharing the Energy

- Each group of dancers will perform its study. The studies should be performed in silence so that the movement alone builds the energy.
- Discuss the energy and emotions felt while dancing and while watching others' sequences evolve.

Discussion Questions

1. How might we define intensity in movement? Is it the same as energy?
2. Explain what you think Alonzo King meant when he stated that "energy is the texture in between"?
3. What choreographic theme might warrant a gradual increase and then decrease of energy?

Intensity: Increasing and Decreasing Force

STATEMENT OF PERFORMANCE

In groups of six or more, dancers will create an Energy study, evolving energy from stillness to great intensity with an explosion leading finally back to stillness in the end.

Answer each of the following criteria with a yes or no and then score each category from 1 to 5, with 5 being the highest score and 1 the lowest. Use the rubrics to assist in discussion, self-reflection, and assessment of progress in understanding the choreographic concept.

Criteria	**Score** YES	NO
CREATING: PERCEPTUAL SKILLS		
The dancers did the following:		
1. Made clear dynamic-quality selections.	_____	_____
2. Created a five-section study using five dynamic qualities.	_____	_____
3. Changed energy use from stillness to maximum activity to stillness once again.	_____	_____
Creating: Perceptual Skills Total	__________	
PERFORMING: TECHNICAL AND EXPRESSIVE SKILLS		
The dancers did the following:		
1. Accurately reproduced selected movement.	_____	_____
2. Performed the same movements with individual timing.	_____	_____
3. Demonstrated building energy intensity followed by its resolution.	_____	_____
4. Flowed easily from one movement to another.	_____	_____
Performing: Technical and Expressive Skills Total	__________	
RESPONDING: INTELLECTUAL AND REFLECTIVE SKILLS		
The dancers did the following:		
1. Discussed choices.	_____	_____
2. Made informed critical observations of own work.	_____	_____
3. Made informed critical observations of the work of others.	_____	_____
4. Noticed and discussed similarities and differences in the different phrases.	_____	_____
Responding: Intellectual and Reflective Skills Total	__________	

SCORING

5 = Fulfilled all the criteria of creating, performing, and responding in a way that shows a thorough understanding of the skills and concepts to be mastered. Fully participated in the classroom tasks as a performer and as an audience member.

4 = Fulfilled all the criteria but does not yet show a thorough understanding of all skills and concepts. Fully participated in classroom tasks as a performer and as an audience member.

3 = Had difficulty fulfilling the criteria. Was not able to fully complete the assignment. Participated in class but could not complete all tasks as a performer and as an audience member.

2 = Did not complete the assigned work to a satisfactory degree. Did not fully participate as a performer or as an audience member.

1 = Did not participate.

ADDITIONAL COMMENTS

____

____

LESSON 5
PROBLEM SOLVING: CREATING A SMALL-GROUP COMPOSITION

© Jeff Cravotta

Mia Cunningham exhibits a strong, percussive, open shape while the other dancers show a contrasting semiclosed, soft, sustained shape in a section of Alonzo King's *Chants*.

Introductory Statement

The use of energy as a motivator for dance sequences allows dancers to explore how movement may be performed with different nuances that add emotional intensity. Dynamics allow for greater variations in expressiveness. It is this understanding of energy use that makes a dancer into an artist who can communicate emotion to the audience.

In the previous four lessons, dancers explored passive weight that led to heaviness and inertia, expanded and contracted by using light and strong energy, explored the six dynamic qualities, and graduated energy intensity from sustained and weak to percussive and strong in a movement study. In the culminating creative problem for this unit, a small group of dancers will explore the communicative power of energy in original movement studies.

Problem-Solving Preparation

Creativity is a cycle that includes varying levels of energy. The brain produces energy, and the process begins slowly, with an idea that germinates in the mind. To move on, we must research our idea and collect information and images. One idea stimulates another until more ideas flow in and the decision is made to try to create the work. Generally, there is a flurry of activity, trial, and error at a heightened energy until the creative problem is solved and the work is finished. Then the stepping back occurs and we reflect on and edit the creation, until finally the energy subsides and we rest until the next creative effort. In *Dreamer,* Alonzo King shows this process in movement. In this lesson, dancers will select their own cyclical theme to inspire a study using movement qualities that increase and decrease in intensity.

Creating a Small-Group Composition

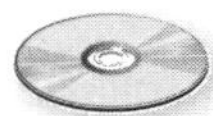

EXAMPLE: Chapter 4, Lesson 5A: Sequence From *Dreamer*

Sattva, or balance and wisdom, enters the space and brings calm to the chaos. He contains the energy and allows it to follow the sequence practiced in lesson 4 of this chapter. Watch how the energy on the stage increases and decreases as the dancers begin slowly and increase their energy to become quick and strong until finally all energy is released into calm.

In a small group of six to eight dancers, select a choreographer. The problem is to create an Energy Evolution study that uses all the material from the preceding lessons. The study should be 3 to 5 minutes long. The choreographer may begin with one or two dancers and add and subtract dancers as the piece proceeds. The dancers may move in unison or separately. The idea is to select a theme that requires the evolution of energy from inertia, or heaviness, through different dynamic qualities to a high point of excitement and then a resolution (see figure 4.3).

One section of composer Alan Hovhaness' *Mysterious Mountain* provides a clear example of growing intensity through volume and the addition of instruments to reach a high point, and then recedes in intensity to calmness. The dance studies will build and recede in a similar fashion. It will be hard to find a musical accompaniment for this study unless a musician is available to improvise or create a score. The study can be performed in silence or with a spoken (words) score that increases in volume along with the dance.

Sample Themes

Stages of development in humans, animals, and birds

Metamorphosis (changing shapes due to growth processes), such as caterpillar to cocoon to butterfly

Human growth cycle from infant to adult to old age

Shape of a day from dawn to noon to dusk to darkness

Rain shower to lightning and thunder to hurricane to wind to rain to stillness

FIGURE 4.3 Sample themes that show an evolution of energy.

Problem Solving: Creating a Small-Group Composition

STATEMENT OF PERFORMANCE

In a small group, the dancers will create an Energy Evolution study that includes dynamic qualities and increases and decreases in intensity. Opening and closing and expanding and contracting will be present in increasing and decreasing intensity.

Answer each of the following criteria with a yes or no and then score each category from 1 to 5, with 5 being the highest score and 1 the lowest. Use the rubrics to assist in discussion, self-reflection, and assessment of progress in understanding the choreographic concept.

Criteria	**Score**	
CREATING: PERCEPTUAL SKILLS	YES	NO
The dancers did the following:		
1. Made clear dynamic-quality selections.	_____	_____
2. Clearly showed an increase and decrease of energy intensity.	_____	_____
3. Made good spatial decisions for the group.	_____	_____
4. Used a specific theme to inform movement choices.	_____	_____
5. Explored expanding and contracting in the group.	_____	_____
Creating: Perceptual Skills Total	__________	
PERFORMING: TECHNICAL AND EXPRESSIVE SKILLS		
The dancers did the following:		
1. Accurately reproduced selected movement.	_____	_____
2. Performed as members of a group, assuming assigned responsibilities.	_____	_____
3. Demonstrated appropriate movement qualities.	_____	_____
4. Showed clear examples of increasing and decreasing intensity.	_____	_____
Performing: Technical and Expressive Skills Total	__________	
RESPONDING: INTELLECTUAL AND REFLECTIVE SKILLS		
The dancers did the following:		
1. Discussed choices.	_____	_____
2. Made informed critical observations of own work.	_____	_____
3. Made informed critical observations of the work of others.	_____	_____
Responding: Intellectual and Reflective Skills Total	__________	

SCORING

5 = Fulfilled all the criteria of creating, performing, and responding in a way that shows a thorough understanding of the skills and concepts to be mastered. Fully participated in the classroom tasks as a performer and as an audience member.

4 = Fulfilled all the criteria but does not yet show a thorough understanding of all skills and concepts. Fully participated in classroom tasks as a performer and as an audience member.

3 = Had difficulty fulfilling the criteria. Was not able to fully complete the assignment. Participated in class but could not complete all tasks as a performer and as an audience member.

2 = Did not complete the assigned work to a satisfactory degree. Did not fully participate as a performer or as an audience member.

1 = Did not participate.

ADDITIONAL COMMENTS

____

____

Student Self-Evaluation Questions

Name: ______________________ Date: ______________ Class: ______________

CREATIVE ASSIGNMENT

1. What was the most interesting aspect of what you did?

2. What was the most challenging problem you had to solve while you were working?

3. How did you try to solve the problem? Describe the process.

4. What did you learn while trying to solve the problem?

5. If you were to repeat this activity again, what would you do differently?

6. What is another project or experience that might grow out of this one?

Choreographic Devices: Creating Finished Compositions

Mia Cunningham finds a moment of stillness during Alonzo King's *Chants*.

OVERVIEW

In the previous chapters of this book, dance compositions were developed from the choreographic operations used by two contemporary choreographers, Alonzo King and Dwight Rhoden. The studies were evolved with the intention of providing movement material for the creation of longer dance choreographies. In this chapter, compositional forms used by King and Rhoden are explored: call and response, canon, AB, ABA, theme and variations, and a suite. These formal structures use material generated in the previous chapters to create more polished compositions.

Creating things and training went hand in hand. They were always together . . . I never did one without the other.

DWIGHT RHODEN, 2003

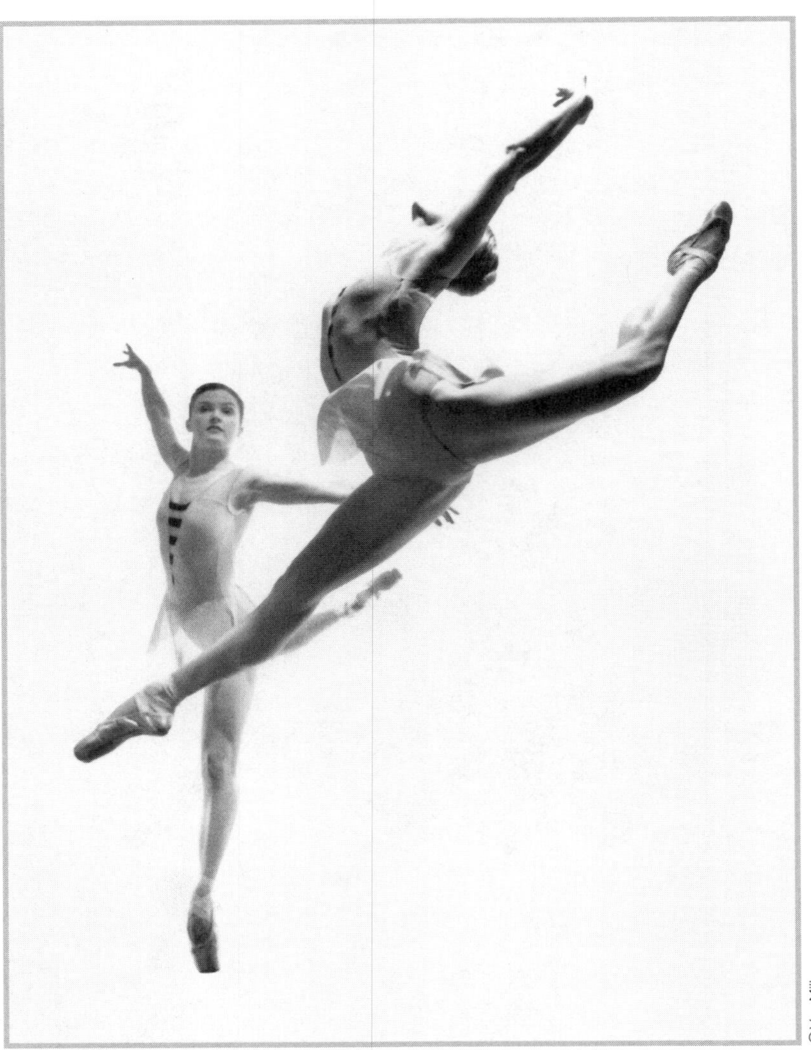

©Van Miller

Amy Earnest and Heather Maloy dance to the call and response chant "Sigereti Fe Bara" from Alonzo King's *Chants*.

The call and response, or antiphon, structure was used by King in *Chants* to coincide with the African songs used as accompaniment. The canon structure was used by both King in *Chants* and Rhoden in *Verge* as a compositional device for a large ensemble of dancers. Both choreographers also created sectional works. *Chants* is a suite of independent dances, each with its own character, and *Verge* is a dance of independent sections, each with a distinct character. Understanding how to create studies with contrasting sections featuring different qualities is an important technique to master. The most elementary exercises in contrast are found while exploring AB compositional forms.

LESSON I
CALL AND RESPONSE: ANTIPHONAL MOVEMENT

Introductory Statement

Call and response, or antiphon, is a structure for composing music and dance that occurs in many cultures, including medieval European and contemporary African cultures. It consists of a leader reciting or dancing a phrase while followers watch and listen. Then the followers repeat the phrase exactly as it was performed by the leader. Choreographer Alonzo King used this structure in *Chants*. Call and response offers an interesting new way to use the dance phrases created in chapter 1.

Vocabulary

antiphonal
call and response
challenge
duet
hocket
phrase
retrograde

Warm-Up and Concept Presentation

- Participate in a call and response word game, for example, the Yoruba chant "Che, Che Kule" (see figure 5.1), or create a rhythmic clapping pattern. Once the pattern is learned, improvise movement with a leader and responders. Explore clapping and movement.
- Discuss call and response and its variation, the hocket (hiccup). The hocket allows the melody to be interrupted by the insertion of rests in such a way that another voice supplies the missing notes. The melody or phrase is divided between the voices.

EXAMPLE: Chapter 5, Lesson 1A: Call and Response Duet

Watch this call and response duet, performed by Amy Earnest and Heather Maloy, from a performance of Alonzo King's *Chants*. The structure of the duet is similar to the creative problem posed in this lesson.

Problem Solving

- Think about reasons for using call and response as a compositional form. Perhaps two people are arguing or telling a funny story, or a teacher is demonstrating to a student how to do something new. In *Chants* the call and response is a challenge game between two dancers to see who will dance the best. The

Call and Response Chant

CHE (chay), CHE, KU - LE (koolay)

1 2 3 4

CHE, CHE, KO VI - SA

1 & (2 Rest) & 3 4

KO VI- SA LAN-GAN

1 & (2 Rest) & 3 4

LAN - GAN CHE LAN GAN

1 & (2 Rest) & 3 4

KOO, A LAY LAY

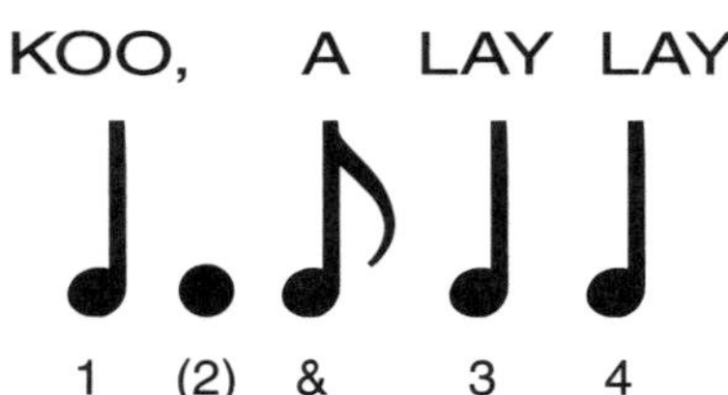

1 (2) & 3 4

KOO, A LAY LAY

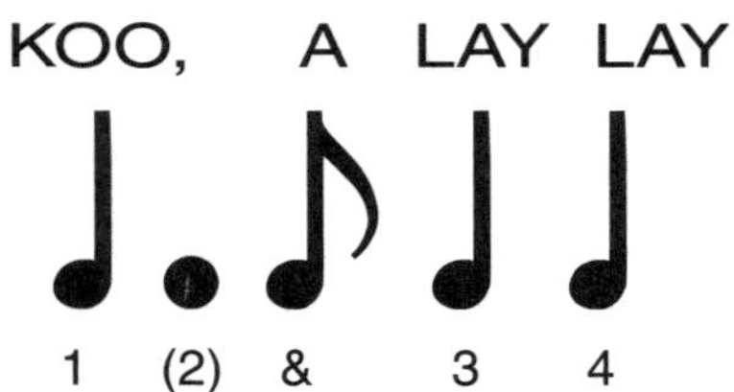

1 (2) & 3 4

FIGURE 5.1 An African call and response chant, "Che, Che, Kule."

movements are quick and difficult, and the dancers begin on cue. Find a theme to inspire original movement choices for call and response.

- In pairs, create a phrase of movement inspired by lesson 2 or lesson 3 from chapter 1. The phrase should be 16 counts (phrase A). Learn and rehearse the phrase together.
- Vary this phrase either by performing it in retrograde or reordering it so that another 16-count phrase evolves (phrase A^1). These two phrases will become the core movement material for the call and response.
- The beginning shape has both dancers in the performing space, but apart.
    1. Complete phrase A performed by dancer 1 (16 counts)
    2. Complete phrase A performed by dancer 2 (16 counts)
    3. Complete reordered or retrograded phrase A^1 performed by dancer 1 (16 counts)
    4. Complete reordered or retrograded phrase A^1 performed by dancer 2 (16 counts)
    5. First half of phrase A performed by dancer 1 (8 counts)
    6. Second half of phrase A performed by dancer 2 (8 counts)
    7. Unison performance of complete phrase A^1 (16 counts)
- The ending shape has both dancers together.
- While one dancer is dancing, the other should simply watch or assume a shape.
- Follow the sequence of the dance and create an original duet.
- Find appropriate music to accompany your work. It does not have to be a call and response; it simply needs a strong pulse.
- Perform finished duets and discuss the choices made for phrases A and A^1. Give feedback about movement choices and execution.

Call and Response: Antiphonal Movement

STATEMENT OF PERFORMANCE

Dancers will perform a duet based upon the call and response compositional form, using original movement phrases.

Answer each of the following criteria with a yes or no and then score each category from 1 to 5, with 5 being the highest score and 1 the lowest. Use the rubrics to assist in discussion, self-reflection, and assessment of progress in understanding the choreographic concept.

Criteria	**Score**	
CREATING: PERCEPTUAL SKILLS	YES	NO
The dancers did the following:		
1. Made good choices in timing and transitions.	_____	_____
2. Followed the assignment accurately.	_____	_____
3. Collaborated with a partner to construct the study.	_____	_____
4. Successfully determined placement in space and beginning and ending shapes.	_____	_____
5. Used the same movement material in phrases A and A[1].	_____	_____
Creating: Perceptual Skills Total	__________	
PERFORMING: TECHNICAL AND EXPRESSIVE SKILLS		
The dancers did the following:		
1. Accurately reproduced selected movement.	_____	_____
2. Clearly demonstrated call and response.	_____	_____
3. Flowed easily from one movement to another.	_____	_____
Performing: Technical and Expressive Skills Total	__________	
RESPONDING: INTELLECTUAL AND REFLECTIVE SKILLS		
The dancers did the following:		
1. Discussed choices.	_____	_____
2. Made informed critical observations of own work.	_____	_____
3. Made informed critical observations of the work of others.	_____	_____
Responding: Intellectual and Reflective Skills Total	__________	

SCORING

5 = Fulfilled all the criteria of creating, performing, and responding in a way that shows a thorough understanding of the skills and concepts to be mastered. Fully participated in the classroom tasks as a performer and as an audience member.

4 = Fulfilled all the criteria but does not yet show a thorough understanding of all skills and concepts. Fully participated in classroom tasks as a performer and as an audience member.

3 = Had difficulty fulfilling the criteria. Was not able to fully complete the assignment. Participated in class but could not complete all tasks as a performer and as an audience member.

2 = Did not complete the assigned work to a satisfactory degree. Did not fully participate as a performer or as an audience member.

1 = Did not participate.

ADDITIONAL COMMENTS

____

____

LESSON 2
CANON: DANCING IN UNISON A FEW COUNTS APART

Vocabulary

canon
round
unison

Introductory Statement

Choreographers use formal structure to add unity to a dance composition just as musicians, painters, and writers use formal structure to add unity to their creations. Formal structures in dance allow a viewer to follow the course of the movement and the line of action throughout a given work. There are many compositional configurations. Some have already been studied, such as the AB form, theme and variation, accumulation, and call and response. The canon uses exact repetition of movement material but varies it by overlapping the beats in the same phrase. In dance, the first performer starts the phrase, or voice, as it is called when the form is applied to music. The second dancer performs the exact same phrase but starts a few beats later than the first one. This overlapping creates interesting new spatial relationships.

Warm-Up and Canon

- Create a new list of nonlocomotor action words similar to the list created in chapter 1, lesson 2, or the list in figure 5.2. Design a phrase of movement that is counted and clearly represents the word list. The phrase should be approximately

© Rolland Elliott

Dancers in Dwight Rhoden's *Verge* demonstrate three separate voices in a movement canon. The women in the center are voice 1, the men on stage left are voice 2, and the men on stage right are voice 3.

32 counts and does not need locomotor movement. Practice the phrase with a partner starting 4 counts apart.

- Create a list of locomotor movement words (see figure 5.3), and create a movement phrase of 16 counts. The phrase should include a direction change with level change. With the same partner, move across the floor 4 counts apart.

Nonlocomotor Action Words

Stretch	Rise	Twist
Contract	Swing	Collapse
Reach	Press	Expand
Melt		

FIGURE 5.2 Create a similar list of movement words; then create a 32-count movement phrase based on your list.

Locomotor Action Words

Slide	Roll	Glide
Leap	Hover	Jump
Skip		

FIGURE 5.3 Create a similar list of movement words; then create a 16-count movement phrase based on your list.

Problem Solving

EXAMPLE: Chapter 5, Lesson 2A: Canon From *Verge*

"Nirvana," the final section of Dwight Rhoden's *Verge*, begins in canon, 4 counts apart. Notice how you as a viewer are pulled into the action that occurs in waves of overlapping movement.

Canon in Four

In groups of four, create a canon of combined nonlocomotor and locomotor movement. Design an interesting starting shape and then perform the canon two by two. The canon should start 4 counts apart. Accompanying music does not have to be in canon. The structure of the dance can be different than the structure of the music. See figure 5.4 for a sample canon.

Tightening the Canon

After performing the canon with a 4-count difference, try the canon with a 2-count difference. Is this harder to perform? How will the spatial relationships change?

Final Form

- Rehearse the Canon studies a final time. One of the dancers will assume the role of the choreographer. The Canon study should include the following:

1. A beginning shape
2. A nonlocomotor phrase of 32 counts (section A)
3. A locomotor phrase of 16 counts (section B)
4. A 4-count lead between voices
5. Both unison and canon phrases as needed for transitions
6. A definite ending either shown by a group shape or exit from the stage area

Sample Canon

1. = performer 1   2. = performer 2   3. = performer 3   4. = performer 4

I.
1. Row, row, row your boat
2. silent
3. silent
4. silent

II.
1. gently down the stream
2. Row, row, row your boat
3. silent
4. silent

III.
1. merrily, merrily, merrily, merrily
2. gently down the stream
3. Row, row, row your boat
4. silent

IV.
1. life is but a dream.
2. merrily, merrily, merrily, merrily
3. gently down the stream
4. Row, row, row your boat

V.
1. silent
2. life is but a dream.
3. merrily, merrily, merrily, merrily
4. gently down the stream

VI.
1. silent
2. silent
3. life is but a dream.
4. merrily, merrily, merrily, merrily

VII.
1. silent
2. silent
3. silent
4. life is but a dream.

FIGURE 5.4 "Row, Row, Row Your Boat" as a canon in four.

- The choreographer should determine how many times each section will be danced and by whom.
- The canon may be performed in pairs (two voices) or as solos (four voices). The choice is up to the choreographer.
- Each quartet should find music. Each group should have discussed a theme that helped to inform the movement choices of the central phrases.
- The Canon studies should be performed for peers, who should provide feedback.

Tightening the Form

Repeat the previous canon, now with a 2-count lead between each voice. Compare the look of both canons.

Canon: Dancing in Unison a Few Counts Apart

STATEMENT OF PERFORMANCE

In quartets, dancers will create an original dance study in canon. They will first perform it with a 4-count lead and then repeat it with a 2-count lead.

Answer each of the following criteria with a yes or no and then score each category from 1 to 5, with 5 being the highest score and 1 the lowest. Use the rubrics to assist in discussion, self-reflection, and assessment of progress in understanding the choreographic concept.

Criteria	**Score**	
CREATING: PERCEPTUAL SKILLS The dancers did the following:	YES	NO
1. Created a 32-count nonlocomotor phrase and a 16-count locomotor phrase.	_____	_____
2. Created a canon with two groups performing 4 counts apart.	_____	_____
3. Included an ending shape with one group finishing first and waiting for the rest.	_____	_____
4. Successfully repeated the canon with a 2-count lead.	_____	_____
Creating: Perceptual Skills Total	_____________	
PERFORMING: TECHNICAL AND EXPRESSIVE SKILLS The dancers did the following:		
1. Accurately reproduced selected movement.	_____	_____
2. Retained strong focus throughout the performance.	_____	_____
3. Presented the canon form clearly.	_____	_____
Performing: Technical and Expressive Skills Total	_____________	
RESPONDING: INTELLECTUAL AND REFLECTIVE SKILLS The dancers did the following:		
1. Discussed choices.	_____	_____
2. Made informed critical observations of own work.	_____	_____
3. Made informed critical observations of the work of others.	_____	_____
Responding: Intellectual and Reflective Skills Total	_____________	

SCORING

5 = Fulfilled all the criteria of creating, performing, and responding in a way that shows a thorough understanding of the skills and concepts to be mastered. Fully participated in the classroom tasks as a performer and as an audience member.

4 = Fulfilled all the criteria but does not yet show a thorough understanding of all skills and concepts. Fully participated in classroom tasks as a performer and as an audience member.

3 = Had difficulty fulfilling the criteria. Was not able to fully complete the assignment. Participated in class but could not complete all tasks as a performer and as an audience member.

2 = Did not complete the assigned work to a satisfactory degree. Did not fully participate as a performer or as an audience member.

1 = Did not participate.

ADDITIONAL COMMENTS

____

____

____

LESSON 3
DIRECTIONAL MIRRORING: PARALLEL REFLECTING AND REVERSE REFLECTING

Vocabulary

duplicitous
facing
glide reflection
irony
locomotor movement
mirroring
pathway
quartet
reflection
symmetry
unison

Introductory Statement

When choreographing a dance, a choreographer must use elements of choreographic forms and techniques of movement development to create unity in the composition. If a choreographer introduces a compositional device, such as mirroring, as an important part of the choreography, it ought to reappear and be developed throughout the work. In the quartet assignment for this lesson, mirroring movement as well as a mirroring pathway on the floor are combined to create a challenging task for the choreographer. The symmetry of the floor design and the symmetry of pairs of dancers reflecting each other's movements will provide a visual balance and a solid compositional structure.

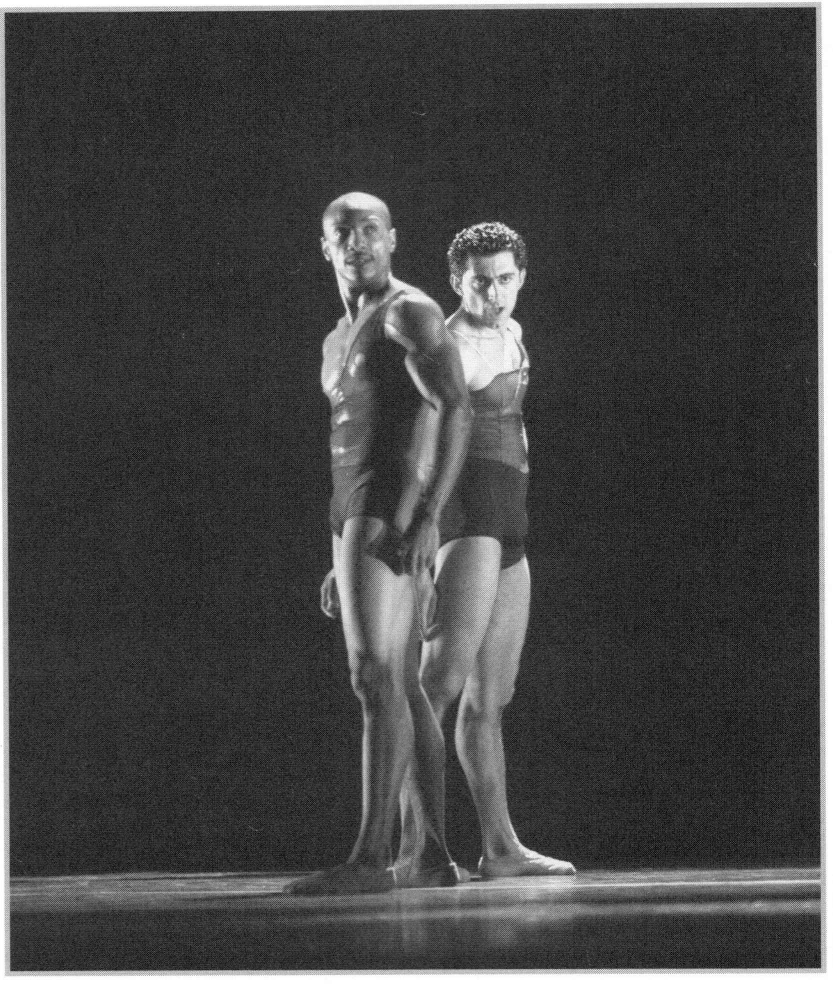

© Rolland Elliott

Uri Sands and Edgar Vardanian pose back to back before assuming their mirroring duet in a moment from *Verge*.

Warm-Up With Mirroring

• Dancers will participate in a mirroring warm-up that may include material from lesson 3 in chapter 2 or may just involve having fun following a leader. Find a partner and explore the unison mirroring of nonlocomotor movement. Change levels and vary tempos.

• Now explore locomotor movement reflections. Face your partner and move slowly at first to ensure that the pathways chosen are exactly the same on both sides of the reflection line. Refer to chapter 2, lesson 6.

Problem Solving

Reflection and Its Glide

• A choreographer chosen from the class will select four dancers and create a Reflection Quartet for them. Construct the quartet by using gesture material translated through the body and performed in unison. Divide the dancers into two pairs on either side of a reflecting line so that one pair of dancers will mirror the other. Find a theme that can provide ample inspiration for the movement phrases.

• The first section should be at least four 8-count phrases of nonlocomotor movement. Include level changes, direction changes, facing changes, and dynamic changes. The dancers may face in whatever direction the choreographer chooses, but the location of the reflecting line must be clear.

• The choreographer will then create at least four new 8-count locomotor phrases that move along a predetermined pathway throughout the space. It might be helpful to draw the pathway on paper for clarity. See figure 5.5 for a sample reflection pathway. The pathway must be the same on both sides of the reflecting line. The movements should also be mirroring.

• The last phrase should repeat the original nonlocomotor material with a change of facing. An example quartet structure:

A (nonlocomotor mirroring movement with different facings, such as side by side or back to back)

B (locomotor movement following a mirrored pathway)

A (nonlocomotor mirrored movement)

Reflection Quartet

A further expansion of this study might follow a script such as this one:

• Symmetrical starting shape.

• Eight measures (4 counts each). All four dancers will use nonlocomotor mirroring, sometimes dancing in pairs, sometimes all together. Dancers connect elbows and hands while sharing weight.

• Eight measures (4 counts each). The two outside partners mirror each other with simple locomotor movement while the two inside partners mirror each other with nonlocomotor movement.

• Eight measures (4 counts each). The two inside partners begin locomotor movement around the outside partners, who are doing nonlocomotor movement.

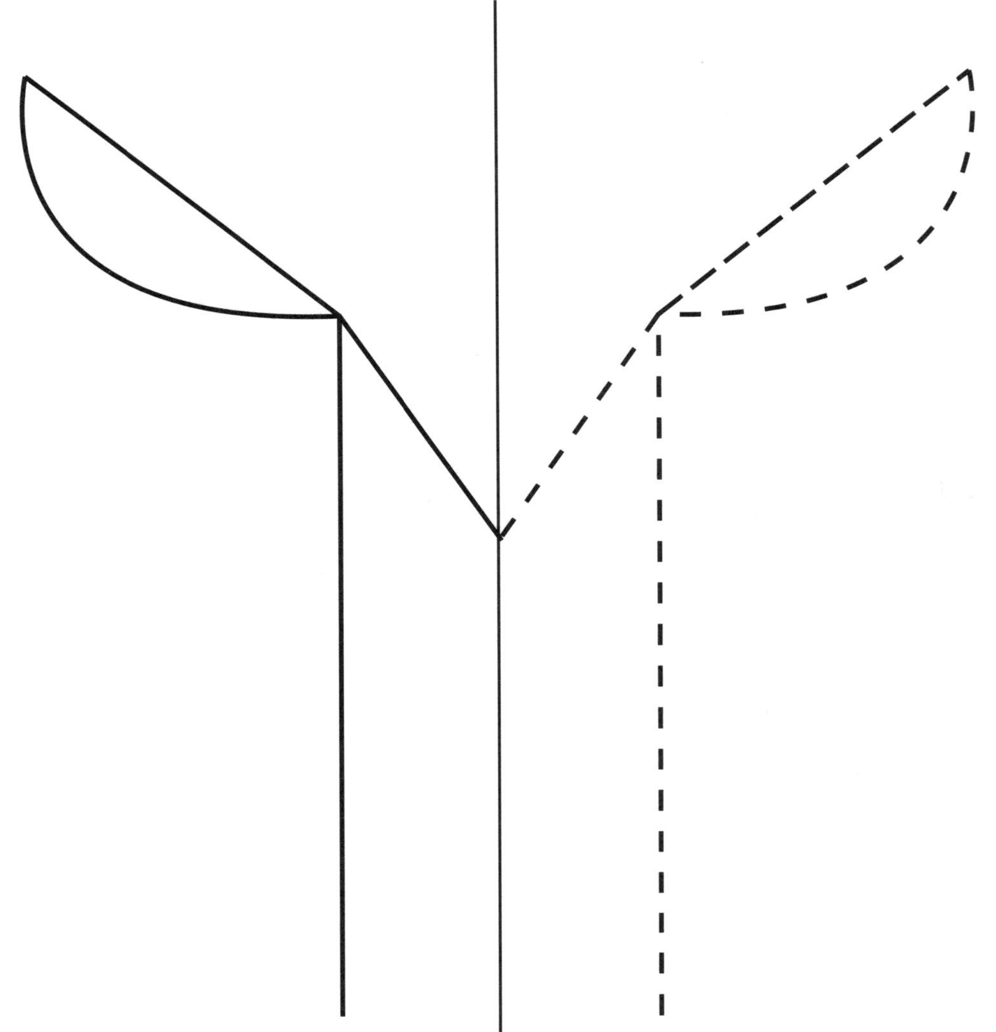

FIGURE 5.5 Sample reflection pathway.

- Eight measures (4 counts each). All four dancers move in reflection pathways covering the full stage.
- Eight measures will be used to explore weight sharing and balances, with pairs on opposite sides of the stage.
- Eight measures (4 counts each) will contain variations of the first 8 measures with couples once again connecting with nonlocomotor mirroring.
- Symmetrical ending shape.

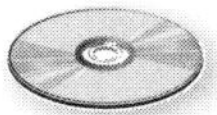

EXAMPLE: Chapter 5, Lesson 3A: Duplicitous Ironies

Heather Ferranti, Nicholle-Rochelle, Jason Jacobs, and Patrick Kastoff perform a reflected quartet from Dwight Rhoden's *Verge*. Note the vertical reflection line that divides the stage into right and left halves. Watch the mirroring variations that occur in both nonlocomotor and locomotor movements.

- Each quartet should perform their work for the others and then discuss their process of creating the work.

Directional Mirroring: Parallel Reflecting and Reverse Reflecting

STATEMENT OF PERFORMANCE

In quartets, dancers will create a Reflection Quartet. Each quartet will separate into pairs to reflect each other.

Answer each of the following criteria with a yes or no and then score each category from 1 to 5, with 5 being the highest score and 1 the lowest. Use the rubrics to assist in discussion, self-reflection, and assessment of progress in understanding the choreographic concept.

Criteria	**Score**	
CREATING: PERCEPTUAL SKILLS The choreographer did the following:	YES	NO
1. Created a clear four-person symmetrical beginning shape.	_____	_____
2. Included 8 measures of 4 counts each of nonlocomotor movement performed in mirrored duets.	_____	_____
3. Included 8 measures of 4 counts each of connected locomotor phrases performed by two dancers on the outside, with inside dancers following. Then reversed the dancers.	_____	_____
4. Included 8 measures of nonlocomotor phrases using weight sharing.	_____	_____
5. Created a four-person mirrored symmetrical ending shape.	_____	_____
Creating: Perceptual Skills Total	__________	
PERFORMING: TECHNICAL AND EXPRESSIVE SKILLS The dancers did the following:		
1. Accurately reproduced selected movement.	_____	_____
2. Mirrored carefully.	_____	_____
3. Retained strong focus throughout the performance.	_____	_____
4. Smoothly transitioned between sections.	_____	_____
Performing: Technical and Expressive Skills Total	__________	
RESPONDING: INTELLECTUAL AND REFLECTIVE SKILLS The dancers did the following:		
1. Discussed choices.	_____	_____
2. Made informed critical observations of own work.	_____	_____
3. Made informed critical observations of the work of others.	_____	_____
Responding: Intellectual and Reflective Skills Total	__________	

SCORING

5 = Fulfilled all the criteria of creating, performing, and responding in a way that shows a thorough understanding of the skills and concepts to be mastered. Fully participated in the classroom tasks as a performer and as an audience member.

4 = Fulfilled all the criteria but does not yet show a thorough understanding of all skills and concepts. Fully participated in classroom tasks as a performer and as an audience member.

3 = Had difficulty fulfilling the criteria. Was not able to fully complete the assignment. Participated in class but could not complete all tasks as a performer and as an audience member.

2 = Did not complete the assigned work to a satisfactory degree. Did not fully participate as a performer or as an audience member.

1 = Did not participate.

ADDITIONAL COMMENTS

____

____

LESSON 4
VARIATION: INTERWEAVING AND VARYING PATTERNS

Vocabulary

brainstorming
retrograde
variations

Introductory Statement

In this choreographic assignment, dancers will design the stage space in the same way a landscape painter might approach a painting. Six dancers will create five independent movement phrases and place them on the stage following a predetermined pathway map. As the dancers meet or their paths cross in space, relationships form, some by accident, some planned. The dance becomes a moving landscape on the stage.

Warm-Up and Brainstorming

Get into groups of six. Review the paintings of Mondrian, Pollock, and Kandinsky studied in chapter 2, lesson 1. Find additional paintings of interest. Choose three works to inspire a dance. You will not be re-creating the paintings but rather will be using the paintings as inspiration. For this assignment one dancer will be the choreographer and five will be dancers.

Mia Cunningham and the women of North Carolina Dance Theatre move together in varied spatial pathways in Alonzo King's *Chants*.

Structured Improvisation

• The designated choreographer and the five dancers will make five independent locomotor phrases inspired by the chosen paintings and their spatial patterning. Each phrase should use its own set of movements tailored to the dancer who will perform them. Each phrase should last 16 counts. Each dancer should be able to repeat the phrase and perform it in retrograde or reorder it.

• While the dancers rehearse their phrases, the choreographer should construct a pathway map indicating entrances and exits and note the use of the stage space. Refer to the different pathway charts provided with this lesson (see figure 5.6). They are actual examples of the pathways used in *Chants.*

Problem Solving

Interweaving Patterns

• The choreographer should place the phrases in the stage space, choosing carefully the spot for each entrance and exit. The choreographer will determine the order of each entrance and design the intersecting pathways and the interaction of dancers as they meet. Each dancer should enter and exit more than once, each time with a variation of the original material.

• At some point, all dancers should come together on the stage and finish in a final shape that reflects the inspiration painting.

• The designated choreographer will decide on the music or accompaniment for the study.

• Videotape the dance during rehearsals and discuss the interweaving relationships.

In the Landscape

• Each quintet will perform the Interweaving Patterns dance for an audience. The paintings used as inspiration should also be made available during the discussion after the study has been performed.

• Dancers will discuss what they learned while constructing this dance and while viewing themselves performing it on the videotape. They will compare their self-observations with the comments of the audience.

EXAMPLE: Chapter 5, Lesson 4A: Interweaving Patterns

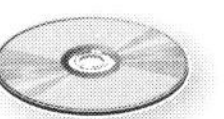

In *Chants,* Alonzo King painted a moving landscape. In the section, "Coconut Pickers Song," seven dancers enter and exit the stage at different times and with different movement phrases. Sometimes the dancers dance independent lines of movement. They rarely interact with each other; rather, they interact with the space. The movement landscape is reminiscent of a watering hole on an African savanna. It is morning and each animal or group of animals arrives, takes a drink, and moves on.

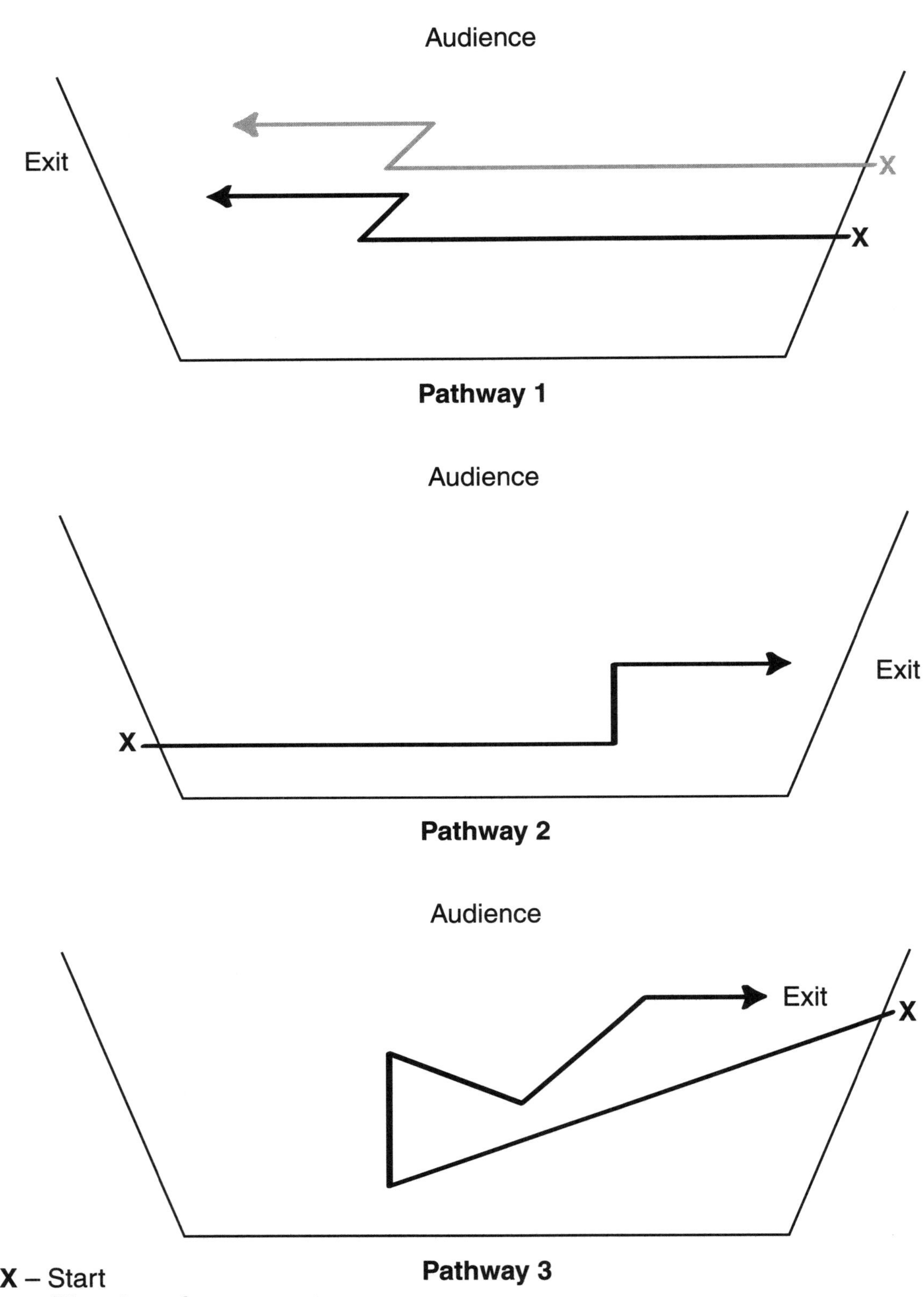

FIGURE 5.6 Sample pathway charts.

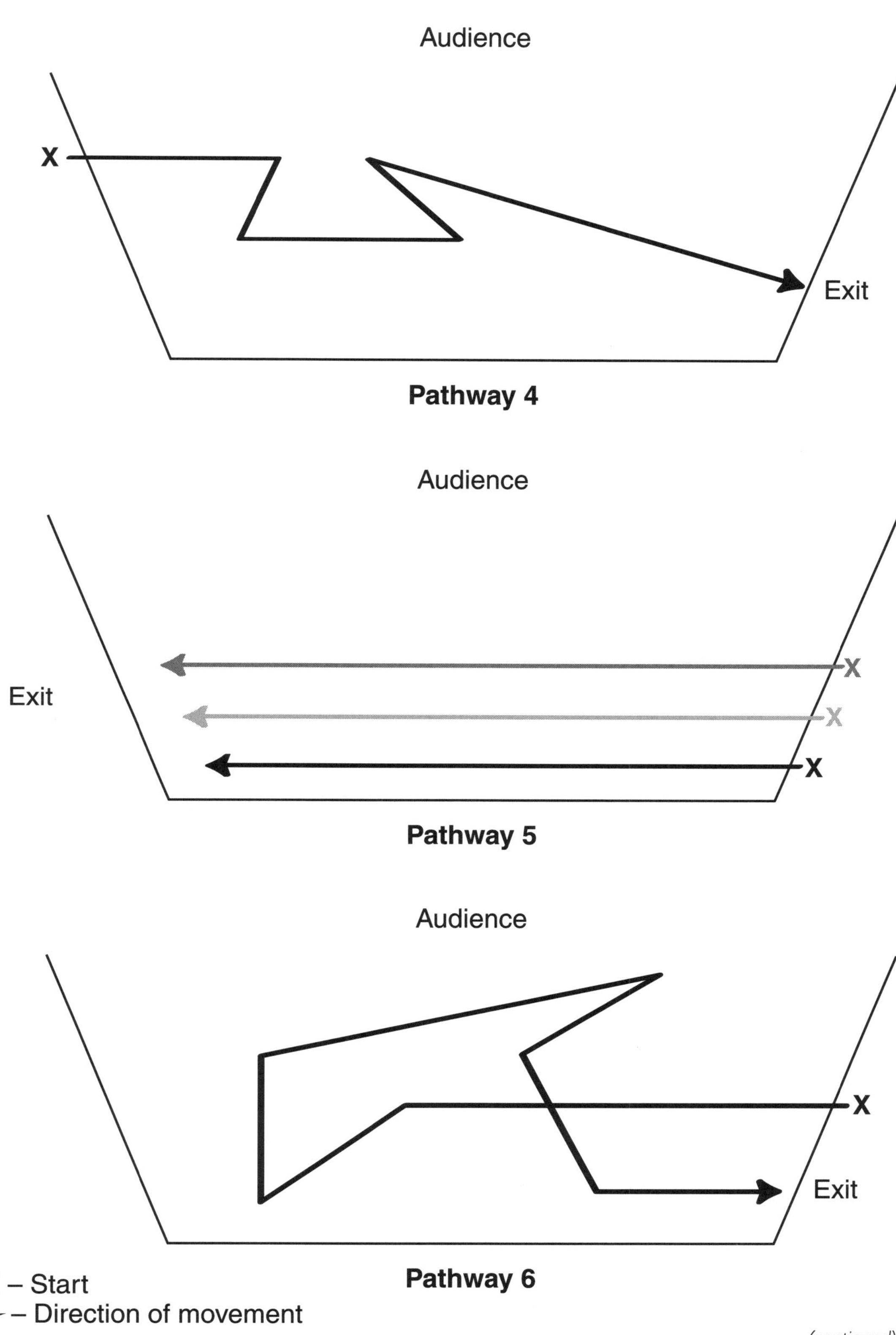

(continued)

FIGURE 5.6 *(continued)*

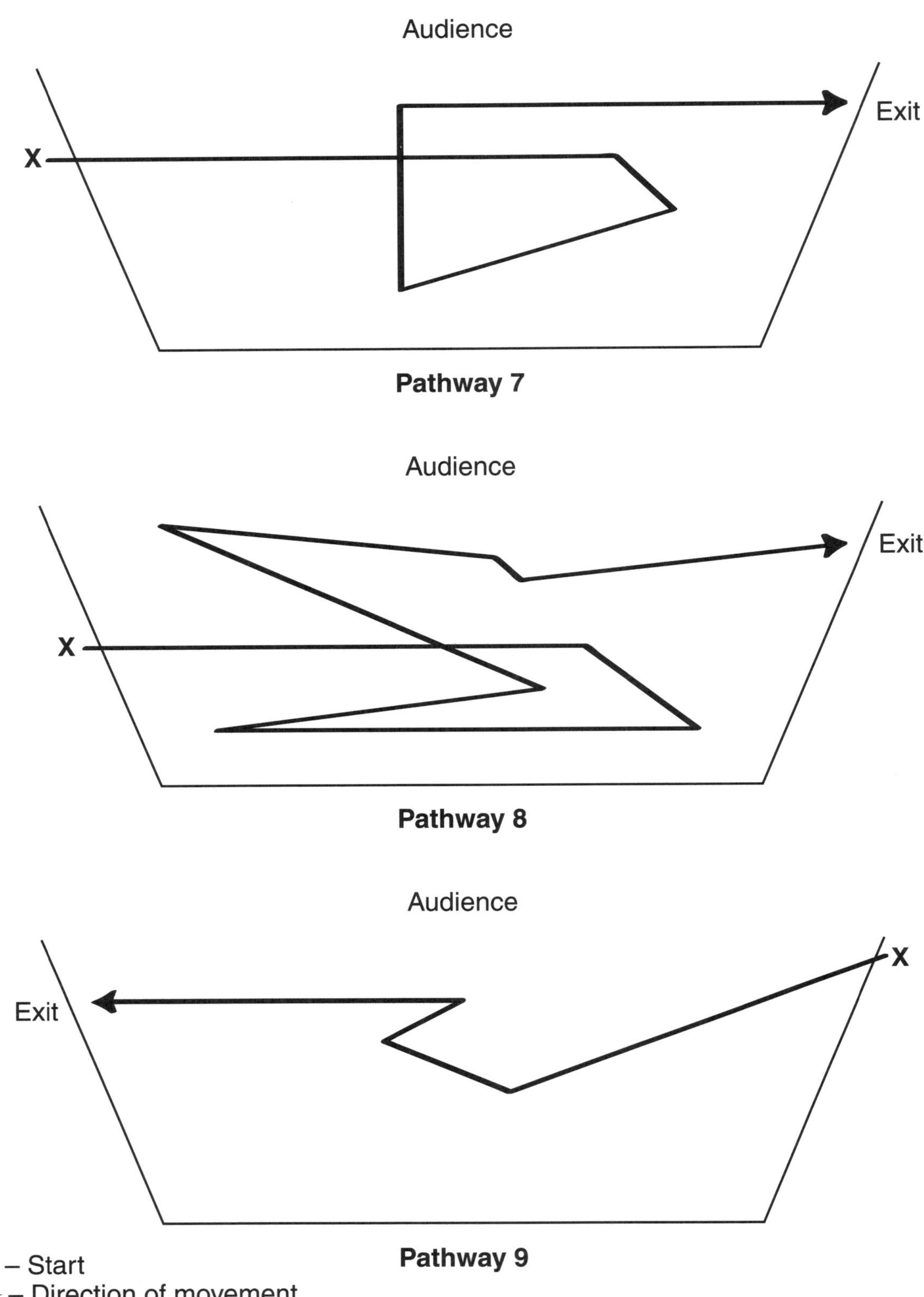

FIGURE 5.6 *(continued)*

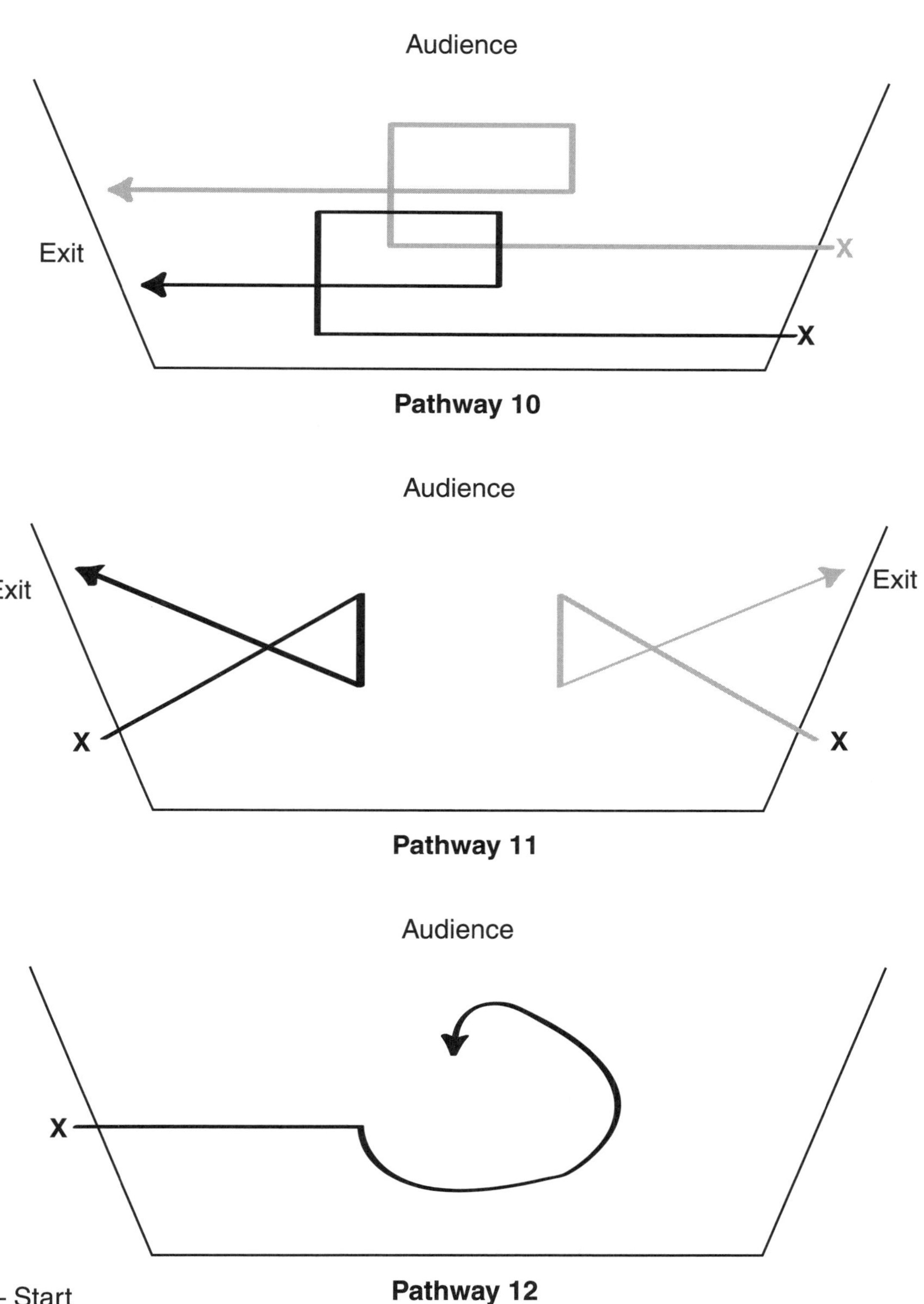

FIGURE 5.6 *(continued)*

Variation: Interweaving and Varying Patterns

STATEMENT OF PERFORMANCE

In groups of six, dancers will create and perform a dance landscape exploring the use of pathways inspired by selected landscape paintings.

Answer each of the following criteria with a yes or no and then score each category from 1 to 5, with 5 being the highest score and 1 the lowest. Use the rubrics to assist in discussion, self-reflection, and assessment of progress in understanding the choreographic concept.

Criteria	**Score** YES	NO
CREATING: PERCEPTUAL SKILLS		
The choreographer and dancers did the following:		
1. Created original phrases with good choices in timing and transitions.	_____	_____
2. Created five independent movement phrases.	_____	_____
3. Created a visual landscape on the stage with varied pathways.	_____	_____
4. Repeated each phrase at least once in a variation (retrograde or reordered).	_____	_____
5. Created a logical ending that evolved out of the interweaving phrases.	_____	_____
Creating: Perceptual Skills Total	__________	
PERFORMING: TECHNICAL AND EXPRESSIVE SKILLS		
The dancers did the following:		
1. Accurately reproduced selected movement.	_____	_____
2. Flowed easily from one movement to another.	_____	_____
3. Clearly danced their pathways.	_____	_____
Performing: Technical and Expressive Skills Total	__________	
RESPONDING: INTELLECTUAL AND REFLECTIVE SKILLS		
The dancers did the following:		
1. Discussed choices.	_____	_____
2. Made informed critical observations of own work.	_____	_____
3. Made informed critical observations of the work of others.	_____	_____
4. Assessed and improved work after seeing it on video.	_____	_____
Responding: Intellectual and Reflective Skills Total	__________	

SCORING

5 = Fulfilled all the criteria of creating, performing, and responding in a way that shows a thorough understanding of the skills and concepts to be mastered. Fully participated in the classroom tasks as a performer and as an audience member.

4 = Fulfilled all the criteria but does not yet show a thorough understanding of all skills and concepts. Fully participated in classroom tasks as a performer and as an audience member.

3 = Had difficulty fulfilling the criteria. Was not able to fully complete the assignment. Participated in class but could not complete all tasks as a performer and as an audience member.

2 = Did not complete the assigned work to a satisfactory degree. Did not fully participate as a performer or as an audience member.

1 = Did not participate.

ADDITIONAL COMMENTS

____

____

LESSON 5
PROBLEM SOLVING: CREATING A MOVEMENT SUITE

© Rolland Elliott

Uri Sands confronting the target from Dwight Rhoden's *Verge.*

Vocabulary

allemande
contrast
courante
duple meter
galliard
gigue
optional dance
pavane
saraband
suite
tempo
theme
triple meter

During the five chapters of this book, dancers have been challenged to reach toward the target of dance composition. In this final assignment, dancers will meet their target like Uri Sands meets the target in *Verge,* with energy and grace, knowing that the end of this journey is near.

Introductory Statement

Historically, the suite was a sectional form of instrumental music that accompanied dance. It consisted of individual, separate pieces, performed one after the other, that were based on the same musical theme and were played in the same key. For the sake of variety, suites followed this pattern: a slow dance (in the Renaissance and earlier times it was called *basse danse)* followed by a faster, jumpy dance *(haute danse).* In the early 17th century, the dances that fitted that mold were the *pavane,* in slow duple meter, and the *galliard,* in fast triple meter. By the end of the 17th century, the suite followed this highly stylized schema:

Allemande (moderate tempo, in 4/4)
Courante (moderately fast, in 6/4)
Saraband (very slow, in 3/4)
Gigue (very fast, in 6/8, compound time)

Often different dances, also called optional dances, were included between the four basic dances. Such dances included the *minuet* (3/4), *gavotte* (2/4), and *bourree* (2/4), among others.

The convention for presenting the overall form of each dance was as follows: A (the first section of the piece, presenting the theme) followed by B (the second section, which developed in a contrasting way to theme A). Therefore, the scheme read as AB. Often each section was repeated as AABB. Sections A and B might have the same number of musical measures, or B could have a few more musical measures. Throughout the lessons in this book, dancers have used AB form and contrasting movement materials to build their studies, such as in chapter 2, lesson 2; chapter 3, lesson 4; and chapter 4, lesson 2.

After 1750 the traditional Baroque suite became extinct. It was absorbed by common classical forms such as the divertimento, cassation, and sonata. Revivals of the suite as a musical form occurred in the late 19th century and even reappeared in the 20th century. In dance, suites are often used by contemporary choreographers who wish to create abstract, sectional dance works. Alonzo King's *Chants* is an example of a work in suite form. The work is accompanied by different African songs and chants. The order of the songs and the dance sections were chosen by King and reflect contrasting tempos and qualities. The sections are quite different from each other and they feature anything from large-group dances with many voices accompanying the movement, to solos and duets with only one or two singers.

Following the form of the dance suite and inspired by *Chants,* dancers will create group works that are made up of two to four independent contrasting sections, alternating slow and fast. Each section should use movement phrases and dynamics and groupings that are different from the previous section.

The work should have a central theme to guide movement choices, but the theme can be abstract or nonliteral such as colors, environments, animals, birds, or creatures in the sea.

Problem Solving

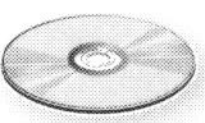

EXAMPLE: Chapter 5, Lesson 5A: Suite From *Chants* (Excerpts)

Included in this example are four sections from Alonzo King's *Chants.* The sections are not in the order of the original dance but have been placed in this order to provide a model for the creative problem that follows. Alonzo King's original suite included 10 different dance sections.

The selected sections are as follows:

- "N'Diouk Tabala Wolof"—A quick men's dance in varied rhythms
- "Yofo Yo"—A weight-sharing, counterbalanced duet for two women
- "N'terole"—A solo featuring acceleration in music and dance
- "Women of Butela"—A quick dance for women, alternating solo with group

• One choreographer will choose a cast of four to six dancers to create a suite of four separate sections. All of the class members should have a role as either choreographer or dancer. If necessary, dancers from outside the class may be used so that all choreographers have four to six dancers as a cast. A movement theme should guide the development of the movement ideas and the choice of music. Each choreographer should use movement material or choreographic operations developed in previous chapters of this book.

Section 1. Quick; full-group dance; duple in 4s.
AB form with two separate types of movement. Choreographers may wish to construct movement sentences of different action words to assure variety.

Section 2. Slow; duet; triple in 3s.
Theme and variations (A, A^1, A^2, A^3, A).
Shapes and sharing weight.

Section 3. Trio; combination of different pulses; duple using half time and double time.
Locomotor and nonlocomotor movement should be designed for each dancer but each dancer should dance to a different beat (pulse, half time, double time).

Section 4. Full group with accelerating and retarding movement; phrases are duple or triple.
Gestures evolve into movement phrases showing different movement qualities. AB form with two types of movement. The theme of the B subsection should take a longer amount of time to complete in order to create a closing for the work. There may be a retard at the end of the work to allow for an ending.

• Assess the process by making a video recording of the work. Watch and critique the work, discussing compositional choices.

Problem Solving: Creating a Movement Suite

STATEMENT OF PERFORMANCE

Dancers will create and perform an original sectional dance work that combines the movement material and ideas previously explored. One choreographer will select dancers and make all artistic choices.

Answer each of the following criteria with a yes or no and then score each category from 1 to 5, with 5 being the highest score and 1 the lowest. Use the rubrics to assist in discussion, self-reflection, and assessment of progress in understanding the choreographic concept.

Criteria	**Score** YES	NO
CREATING: PERCEPTUAL SKILLS		
The choreographer did the following:		
1. Made good choices in timing and transitions.	_____	_____
2. Selected an appropriate guiding idea.	_____	_____
3. Collaborated with the rest of the cast to construct the complete piece.	_____	_____
4. Offered creative suggestions about order and material.	_____	_____
5. Created four contrasting sections of a suite.	_____	_____
Creating: Perceptual Skills Total ___________		
PERFORMING: TECHNICAL AND EXPRESSIVE SKILLS		
The dancers did the following:		
1. Accurately reproduced selected movement.	_____	_____
2. Performed contrasting movement sections correctly.	_____	_____
3. Flowed easily from one movement to another.	_____	_____
Performing: Technical and Expressive Skills Total ___________		
RESPONDING: INTELLECTUAL AND REFLECTIVE SKILLS		
The dancers did the following:		
1. Discussed choices.	_____	_____
2. Made informed critical observations of own work.	_____	_____
3. Made informed critical observations of the work of others.	_____	_____
Responding: Intellectual and Reflective Skills Total ___________		

SCORING

5 = Fulfilled all the criteria of creating, performing, and responding in a way that shows a thorough understanding of the skills and concepts to be mastered. Fully participated in the classroom tasks as a performer and as an audience member.

4 = Fulfilled all the criteria but does not yet show a thorough understanding of all skills and concepts. Fully participated in classroom tasks as a performer and as an audience member.

3 = Had difficulty fulfilling the criteria. Was not able to fully complete the assignment. Participated in class but could not complete all tasks as a performer and as an audience member.

2 = Did not complete the assigned work to a satisfactory degree. Did not fully participate as a performer or as an audience member.

1 = Did not participate.

ADDITIONAL COMMENTS

____

____

____

Student Self-Evaluation Questions

Name: ______________________ Date: ______________ Class: ______________

CREATIVE ASSIGNMENT

1. What is the most interesting aspect of what you did?

2. What was the most challenging problem you had to solve while you were working?

3. How did you try to solve the problem? Describe the process.

4. What did you learn while trying to solve the problem?

5. If you were to repeat this project again, what would you do differently?

6. What is another project or experience that might grow out of this one?

Glossary

abstraction—The expression of a quality apart from an object; the dealing of a subject in its abstract aspects. An abstract ballet may be a composition of pure dance movement without a plot or association of ideas. Plotless ballets of this kind appear mostly in the 20th century. Dwight Rhoden's *Verge* is an abstract ballet.

acceleration—Gradually moving faster.

action—Movement with intent.

action word—Word that motivates or describes movement or defines body shape.

active weight—Use of body weight to add force and strength to movement. Terms used to describe use of active weight are *strong* and *light.*

adagio—Slow and sustained movement.

air pathway—Pathway described in the air surrounding the body.

allegro—Fast movement.

allemande—Dance in duple moderate tempo.

antiphonal—Alternating parts.

asymmetry—Form that is not the same on both sides when divided in half; however, the form may be balanced and visually pleasing because of the tensions of imbalance.

balance—Even distribution of weight; steady position or state.

beat—Regularly recurring unit of musical time; time-force concept representing an amount of force and the movement of time.

beginning shape—Shape or posture a dancer assumes before starting to move, as if waiting for the curtain to go up.

brainstorming—To improvise ideas.

call and response—Structure for composing dance and music that consists of a leader reciting or dancing a phrase while followers watch or listen and then repeat.

canon—Music or dance composition in several voices, each starting at a different time and finishing in the same order at a different time.

carving—Movement that carves space, drawing from the periphery to the center of the body. Usually, the movement is curving.

center of the body—Center of weight in the body, 2 inches below the navel or at the sacrolumbar joint where the weight of the head and torso meet the pelvis and the weight of the upper body is then evenly distributed by the pelvis to the legs. Modern dance training uses the phrase "moving from the center of the body" and emphasizes knowledge of the use of weight distribution throughout the body.

challenge—Contest or dare; one-upmanship.

choreographer—Person who choreographs a dance.

choreography—Art of constructing a dance. Choreography includes developing movement phrases that are sequenced and composed according to established practices and formal structures.

collapse—Release of tension in any part of the body; when gravity takes over. May be slow or sudden.

combination—Selection and ordering of movements into a longer phrase or phrases; combining movements together to form dance phrases.

compound time—Meters in which the basic pulse is divided into three parts, and the counts are phrased in groups of three, such as 6/8 or 9/8.

contract (close)—Become smaller or shorter.

contrast—Degree of difference between tones, color, or movement.

corners—Space between two meeting lines or surfaces. Also called *angles.*

counterbalance—Sharing weight between two dancers so that the center of gravity is between them. If one dancer releases a grip, both will fall.

courante—Quick dance in triple time.

cube—Rectangular six-sided solid body with identical, square sides.

dab—Movement word used to define one of Rudolf Laban's Efforts; a dab is light in force, quick in tempo, and direct in spatial pathway.

dance phrase—Used interchangeably with *sequence* to indicate a series of specific movements.

dancer counts—Counts ascribed to movement. Choreographers and dancers organize dance movements into groups of counts. Dancer counts loosely follow the counting structure of music but often the dance phrases are not the same as the music phrases.

deceleration—Gradually moving slower.

deconstruction—Selecting movements or components from a dance phrase, taking them apart, and putting them back together again.

design—Pattern in space.

diagonal—Straight, oblique line extending between any two nonadjacent angles of a rectilinear figure; stretching from corner to corner.

dimension—Size of a movement.

direct space—Straight lines and angles that are pointed and specific in direction; defines how space is used.

double time—Counting or moving twice as fast as the beat.

duet—Performance piece for two people. In a danced duet the audience is aware of the shared space and shapes made by the two dancers together in time and space.

duple meter—Meters with beats in subdivisions of two or four, such as 2/4 or 4/4.

duplicitous—Deceitful.

dynamic qualities—Shadings of intensity given to movement to provide contrasts and to define subtleties of meaning.

dynamics—Study of the causes of motion.

energy—The force behind movement, generally on a continuum from strong to light; can change the motion, physical composition, or temperature of an object.

environment—Surroundings, especially those affecting people's lives.

expand (open)—To unfold or spread out.

extension—Stretching or lengthening at a joint; associated with hinge joints (knees and elbows).

facing—Direction a dancer faces in space.

fall—Giving in to the force of gravity.

flexible space—Indulgent use of space in curves and twists that is not as specific in direction as direct space; defines how space is used.

flexion—Bending at a joint; associated with hinge joints (knees and elbows).

float—Movement word used to define one of Rudolf Laban's Efforts; a float is light in force, slow in tempo, and indirect in spatial pathway.

floor pathway—Pathway described along the floor, also called a floor pattern; design made on the floor by the dancer during the course of a dance sequence.

focal point—Point of attention. The focus may be in space or internalized.

force—Something that can accelerate an object (push or pull).

formation—Position of a group of dancers in the stage space; shapes that are made when dancers are formed into groups.

galliard—Quick, jumping dance in triple time.

general space—Space throughout a room that is traveled through using pathways (locomotor movement).

geometric figures—Figures in nature that are studied in geometry (e.g., square, cube, triangle, cone).

geometry—Branch of mathematics that deals with the measurement, properties, and relationship of points, lines, angles, surfaces, and solids. Geometric shapes commonly used in dance include the circle, rectangle, square, triangle, figure eight, and parallel lines.

gesture—Movement of the body or limbs that expresses or emphasizes an idea, sentiment, or attitude.

gigue—Quick dance in compound time.

glide—Movement word that is used to define one of Rudolf Laban's Efforts; a glide is light in force, slow in tempo, and direct in spatial pathway.

glide reflection—Reflecting figure that travels in space with its image, keeping the same relationship to the reflecting line; a mirrored pathway.

gravity—Force that attracts bodies toward the center of the earth.

growth—Process of increasing in size or quantity; to become greater; the process of developing.

half time—Counting or moving twice as slow as the beat.

heaviness—Allowing weight to be used passively, sensing the force of gravity pulling the body downward.

hocket—Musical melody interrupted by the insertion of rests in such a way that another voice supplies the missing notes. The melody is divided between two or more voices. Hocket is Latin for "hiccup."

impulse—Energy (emotional or physical) that motivates movement.

inertia—State of being unable to move; resistance to action.

intensity—Employing much effort; strong quality.

intent—Reason, or motivation, that evokes a movement response.

interdependence—Mutually dependent on another dancer, such as is experienced in weight sharing and in supported balances.

interlocking forms—Two different shapes that intertwine and seem as if they are one shape.

interpersonal space—Space shared by two or more objects or persons.

irony—Paradox or deceit.

isolation—Moving one part of the body while others remain still.

levels—Location in space of a movement. Levels are described as high, with feet off the ground as in jumping; middle, with feet on the floor as in walking; or low, with some part of the upper body on the floor.

lifting—When one dancer is raised off the ground by another. The dancer may be carried somewhere else or simply hoisted straight up in the air.

light—Movement that defies gravity. Its emphasis is upward and without effort or weight.

lightness—Carrying the feeling of weight in the upper part of the body; consciously lifting the body weight away from the floor.

locomotor movement—Movement that moves through space from one place to another, such as a walk, run, leap, hop, jump, prance, triplet, skip, slide, or gallop.

mapping skills—The ability to find the most efficient route from one place to another by using a map. Routes of travel are pathways with a beginning point of origin and an ending point, the destination.

mime—To act a part by mimicking gesture and action without words.

mirroring—Movement performed exactly like that of a partner, like an image in a mirror.

motion—Movement in time and space.

movement qualities—Mechanical application and distribution of energy to the moving parts of the body.

negative space—Empty space that contains no object or person.

nonlocomotor movement—Movement that stays in one place (the feet do not move along a floor pathway). Includes body shapes and movement in the torso and arms.

optional dance—Dance not traditionally in a suite but added at the discretion of the choreographer.

pas de deux—Dance for two people.

passive weight—Giving in to gravity; feeling heaviness while moving. Terms used to describe passive weight are *heavy* and *weak.*

pathway—Design of a movement in space; its trail. Pathways have a beginning and ending point. If the beginning point and ending point are the same, the pathway is closed, such as a circle or square. If the beginning and ending points are different, the pathway is open, such as a route description. In dance, pathways may be described in the air or on the ground. They may contain lines that are angular, straight, curved, or twisted.

pavane—Slow dance of presentation and pomp in duple time. The feet remain close to the floor.

percussive—Sharp, aggressive movement as a result of applying sudden force and then quickly checking it.

personal space—The "reach" space around a person when not moving (nonlocomotor movement).

phrase—Series of specific seqenced movements.

positive space—Space that is occupied by an object or person.

potential energy—Energy of a position.

proscenium—Platform of stage; the space between the curtain and the orchestra.

pulse—Succession of underlying impulses often interchanged with beat.

quartet—Dance for four people.

range of motion—The range of movement available around a joint. See also *flexion, extension,* and *rotation.*

reaction—Physical response to a stimulus.

reflection—Exact image of an existing form; to give back an image or picture of an object.

reflection line—Imaginary line that bisects the dance space into two halves. The line may be horizontal (from side to side) or vertical (from top to bottom).

retard (ritardando)—Gradually getting slower.

retrograde—Compositional operation that reverses the order of an established phrase so that it is performed backward.

reverse—Transposed movement from one side of the body to the other; to proceed in a direction opposite to the one previously followed; to turn around.

rise—Lifting the body weight to a higher level or position; to take up from the ground.

rotation—Turning motion of a joint, associated with a ball-and-socket joint (thigh joint, shoulder joint).

round—Another term for a canon; a dance form in a circle.

saraband—Slow, majestic dance in triple time.

sectional—Divided into separate parts.

sequence—Established series of ordered movements that may be repeated.

shape—Outward form of an object. In dance and in geometry the terms *angles, curves, twisted,* and *straight lines* are used to describe shapes in space.

sink—Heavy release of weight toward the floor, usually in slow, sustained movement.

soft—Gentle, often delicate, movement using body weight lightly.

solo—Choreographed dance for one dancer, either alone on stage or performed in the midst of a larger dance section.

space—Area in a personal kinesphere or, in general, the space of a room. Defined by terms such as *planes, pathways,* and *points in space,* space use in dance is described as indirect or direct and flexible or rigid.

spokelike—Movement beginning in the center of the body and piercing outward into space. Usually the movement consists of straight lines and angles.

stimulus—Motivator that results in an action.

street dance—Popular dance forms evolving from the community. Also referred to as *vernacular dance.*

strong—Forceful and weighty use of energy in the body; claiming and using weight actively.

structured improvisation—Planned set of movement problems established by the facilitator to be solved in an improvisational exercise with students.

succession—Wavelike movement starting at one point in the body and moving smoothly from one body part to another. Examples of succession occur through the spine or from one arm to the other.

suite—Sequence of musical or dance pieces.

supporting—Keeping from falling or sinking; holding in position; when dancers are called upon to provide support for another dancer in order for them to balance or assume shapes they could not make alone.

suspended—Movement is suspended when the pull of two opposing forces is even in a moment of stillness before gravity takes over. Suspension occurs at the height of a leap or the topmost point of a swing.

sustained movement—Smooth, even movement as a result of a steady, equalized release of energy.

swing—Slight impulse giving away to gravity to an unchecked follow-through in an arc to a momentary pause before repetition.

symmetry—Beauty of form arising from balanced proportions. Both sides of an object or image correspond in size, shape, and relative proportion when divided in half.

tempo—Rate of speed of the underlying pulse.

tessellation—Mosaic work made up of interlocking shapes.

theme—Subject of a composition; used for the central idea of a dance work and also for the movement vocabulary selected for the work.

time—Rhythmic basis of movement.

transition—Movement between established shapes or movement phrases, or the "glue in the seams" of a dance work; moving from one movement to another or one section of a dance phrase to another.

translation—Choreographic operation that requires a movement, originally performed in one part of the body, to be translated to the whole body and even into space.

triple meter—Beats in subdivisions of three, such as 3/4 or 6/4.

trust exercises—Exercises designed to explore cooperation through weight-sharing activities. One person is passive and relies on a partner or group to control her movement.

undercurve—Shifting weight from one foot to the other by giving in to gravity at the point between the feet. The undercurve makes an arc in space.

unison—All dancers moving together at the same time with the same movement.

unity—Cohesion in compositional structure.

variations—Repeating thematic material in a different form or using different choreographic operations.

vibratory—Quick, recurring succession of small, percussive movements. Energy is applied in brief spurts.

visual balance—Equipoise between contrasting, opposing, or interacting elements; an aesthetically pleasing integration of elements.

warm-up—Series of movement exercises designed to prepare the body for more rigorous movement.

weight—Mass of an object.

weight sharing—Movement activities that allow dancers to give weight to one another and to carry and support each other while moving.

weightlessness—Feeling an absence of gravity in movement.

zigzag—Crisscrossing space from one diagonal to the other in short spurts.

Bibliography

General Resources

Apel, Willi. *Harvard Dictionary of Music.* Cambridge, MA: Harvard University Press, 1953.

Banes, Sally. *Terpsichore in Sneakers.* Hanover, NH: Wesleyan University Press, 1978.

Bauer, Marion, and Ethel Peyser. *Music Through the Ages.* New York: Putnam, 1967.

Csikszentmihaly, Mihaly. *Creativity.* New York: Harper Collins, 1996.

Gardner, Howard. *Frames of Mind: The Theory of Multiple Intelligences.* Scranton, PA: Basic Books, 1983.

Grout, Donald. *A History of Western Music.* New York: Norton, 1960.

Hanna, Judith Lynne. *Partnering Dance and Education.* Champaign, IL: Human Kinetics, 1999.

Hanna, Judith Lynne. *The Performer-Audience Connection.* Austin, TX: University of Texas Press, 1983.

Hodes, Stuart. "Transforming Dance History: The Lost History of Rehearsals." *Design for Arts in Education* 91, no. 2 (1989): 10-17.

Jonas, Gerald. *Dancing: The Pleasure, Power, and Art of Movement.* New York: Harry Abrams, 1998.

Kapit, Wynn, and Lawrence Elson. *The Anatomy Coloring Book.* New York: Barnes and Noble, 1977.

Kaplan, Robert. *Rhythmic Training for Dancers.* Champaign, IL: Human Kinetics, 2002.

Kirsten, Lincoln. *Dance: A Short History of Classical Theatrical Dancing.* New York: Dance Horizons, 1977.

Sorell, Walter. *Dance in Its Time.* New York: Doubleday, 1981.

Sterns, Jean, and Marshall Sterns. *Jazz Dance.* London: Schirmer Books, 1968.

Taylor, Bruce T. *The Arts Equation.* New York: Back Stage Books, 1999.

Dance Composition Resources

Beaumont, Cyril W. *Michael Fokine and His Ballets.* London: Dance Books, 1996.

Cheney, Gay. *Basic Concepts in Modern Dance.* Princeton, NJ: Princeton Book Co., 1989.

Foster, Susan Leigh. *Choreography and Narrative: Ballet's Staging of Story and Desire.* Bloomington, IN: Indiana University Press, 1996.

Hawkins, Alma. *Creating Through Dance.* Princeton, NJ: Princeton Book Co., 1964.

Hayes, Elizabeth. *Dance Composition and Production.* Princeton, NJ: Princeton Book Co., 1993.

Horst, Louis. *Modern Dance Forms.* Princeton, NJ: Princeton Book Co., 1987.

Horst, Louis. *Pre-Classic Dance Forms.* Princeton, NJ: Princeton Book Co., 1987.

Humphrey, Doris. *The Art of Making Dances.* Revised edition. Princeton, NJ: Princeton Book Co., 1987.

Joyce, Mary. *First Steps in Teaching Creative Dance to Children.* Palo Alto, CA: Mayfield, 1973.

Lavender, Larry. *Dancers Talking Dance: Critical Evaluation in the Choreography Class.* Champaign, IL: Human Kinetics, 1996.

Lawson, Joan. *A Ballet-Maker's Handbook: Sources, Vocabulary, Styles.* New York: Theatre Arts Books/Routledge, 1991.

Morgenroth, Joyce. *Dance Improvisations.* Pittsburg, PA: University of Pittsburg Press, 1987.

National Standards for Arts Education. Reston, VA: Music Educators National Conference, 1994.

Web Resources

Alonzo King, Lines Ballet Company: www.linesballet.org

Dwight Rhoden, Complexions Dance Company: www.complexionsdance.org

National Dance Education Organization: www.ndeo.org

North Carolina Dance Theatre: www.ncdance.org

Resources for K-12 Dance Educators and Professional Dance Organizations

National Assessment of Education Program: www.nces.ed.gov/naep

Saskatchewan Arts Education Rubrics: www.sasked.gov.sk.ca/branches/curr/evergreen/index.shtml

Index

Note: Page numbers followed by an italicized *f* or *t* refer to the figure or table on that page, respectively.

About the Author

Pamela Anderson Sofras, MEd, is a professor of dance and dance education at the University of North Carolina. She has 30 years of experience teaching dance at the university level and has taught and developed courses in modern dance technique, composition, dance education methods, and student teaching. From 1978 to 1990, she was affiliated with the American Dance Festival as a faculty member. She served as assistant, associate dean, and founding director of the Young Dancer's School of the American Dance Festival.

Sofras was part of a team of educators who wrote dance education guidelines for training K-12 dance teachers for the public schools of North Carolina. She has also developed curriculum materials, supported by state and national grants, for professional arts organizations located in New Jersey, North Carolina, Tennessee, and New York. Sofras has been the recipient of six North Carolina Arts Council grant awards to study the choreographic processes of five separate choreographers as they created work for North Carolina Dance Theatre, a professional dance company. The processes were documented and translated into curriculum materials for teachers and for university classes.

A charter member of the National Dance Education Organization (NDEO), Sofras is also a member of the education committee of the North Carolina Dance Theatre and a site evaluator for the North Carolina Arts Council grant activities. She has received numerous awards for her contributions to the field of dance education, including the NDEO's Vision Award, the American Alliance for Health, Physical Education, Recreation and Dance (AAHPERD) College/University Educator of the Year, and the North Carolina Dance Alliance Award. In addition, she received the UNC Service Award in 2002 for her sustained service to public schools. Sofras regularly presents professional development workshops in dance pedagogy for teaching artists and teachers working in public and private school settings.